VEGETABLE GARDENER'S BIBLE

[5 Books in 1] Transform Any Space into a Thriving Vegetable Garden • Organic Pest-Free Methods from the Old Farmer's Almanac for a Bountiful Harvest Year-Round

MELANIE J. DAVIS

© Copyright 2023 by Melanie J. Davies - All rights reserved.

All rights reserved. No part of this book may be reproduced in any form without permission in writing from the author. Reviewers may quote brief passages in reviews.

While all attempts have been made to verify the information provided in this publication, neither the author nor the publisher assumes any responsibility for errors, omissions, or contrary interpretation of the subject matter herein.

The views expressed in this publication are those of the author alone and should not be taken as expert instruction or commands. The reader is responsible for his or her own actions, as well as his or her own interpretation of the material found within this publication.

Adherence to all applicable laws and regulations, including international, federal, state and local governing professional licensing, business practices, advertising, and all other aspects of doing business in the US, Canada or any other jurisdiction is the sole responsibility of the reader and consumer.

Neither the author nor the publisher assumes any responsibility or liability whatsoever on behalf of the consumer or reader of this material. Any perceived slight of any individual or organization is purely unintentional.

Table of Contents

FOREWORD 9

BOOK 1: Vegetable Gardening Basics 11

Introduction 13

How to Plan Your Vegetable Garden.. 14
    Location, size and orientation..14
    Structure and fencing 16
  How to prepare your soil... 17
    When to prepare the soil? 18
    First step to prepare the soil 18
    Basic fertilization..19
    Milling...20
    How many and what are the soil types?...20

Choosing & Starting Seeds... 23
  Seed Selection 23
  Seed Starting Methods 24
  How to Collect & Store Seeds 26
    How to harvest seeds from your garden 26
    When to collect seeds? 27
    How to Store Seeds...27
  Soil temperature and seed germination chart 28

Understanding Basic Plant Biology... 29
  How do plants thrive? 31
  Step-by-step nurture process 32
  What about the fertilizer?... 32
  Fertilizer Ratios for Common Vegetables... 33

How to Grow Common Vegetables 35
  Tomatoes 35
  Cucumbers.. 36
  Zucchini 37
  Cauliflower... 38
  Lettuce 40
  Cabbage 41
  Carrots 42

    Celery...44

    Potatoes...46

    Onion...48

How To Diagnose & Solve Common Gardening Issues 50

  How to Avoid Plant Diseases 50

  Plant Diseases By Unwanted Guests 50

  Fungal Plant Diseases 51

  Most Common Pest & Disease 52

  Climatic Conditions Favoring Plant Diseases 53

  Plant Nutritional Deficiencies 53

Conclusion 58

BOOK 2: Organic Vegetable Gardening 59

Introduction 61

Soil Health 62

  How to Analyze your Soil 62

    Simple observation..*62*

    Identifying Wild Grasses...*63*

    The Measurement of Soil pH...*64*

    How to measure pH with a litmus paper...*65*

    Soil Ph levels for plant chart...*67*

  Organic Techniques to Improve Soil Quality 68

    Compost...*68*

    Cover Crops *70*

    Crop Rotation..*71*

Natural Pest & Disease Control 74

  Companion Planting 74

    Benefits of Companion Planting *74*

    Best plant Alliances in Companion Planting *75*

  Beneficial Plant Insects & Their Role 76

    Types of Beneficial Insects *76*

    Functions of Beneficial Insects *76*

    Factors Affecting Beneficial Insect Populations *77*

    How to Promote Beneficial Insect Populations *77*

    Beneficial insect chart...*78*

  Organic Sprays & Dusts 79

Types of Organic Sprays and Dusts 79

Functions of Organic Sprays and Dusts 79

Factors Influencing the Effectiveness 80

Safety Considerations 80

Natural Fertilizers 81

Types of Natural Fertilizers 81

Functions of Natural Fertilizers 81

Factors Influencing the Effectiveness of Natural Fertilizers 82

How to Fertilize Your Vegetable Garden 82

Natural Nutrient Value Chart 84

Sustainable Practices 85

Rainwater Harvesting 85

Benefits of Rainwater Harvesting 85

Getting Started with Rainwater Harvesting 86

Maintenance of Rainwater Harvesting Systems 86

Greywater Recycling 87

Step-by-Step Guide to Greywater Recycling 87

Benefits of Greywater Recycling 87

Permaculture Design 88

The Principles of Permaculture Design 88

How to Apply Permaculture Design 89

Conclusion 90

BOOK 3: Growing Vegetables in Container 91

Introduction 93

The Benefits of Container Gardening 94

Container Selection and Preparation 95

Dimension 95

Pot Shape 95

Materials 96

Drainage 97

Saucer 98

Vegetable Container Gardening Chart Guide 99

Common Vegetables & How to Grow Them 100

Tomatoes 100

Peppers 100

- Lettuce 101
- Spinach 101
- Cucumbers 102
- Zucchini 102
- Carrots 103
- Radishes 103
- Beets 104

Container Gardening Techniques 105
- The Ideal Potting Soil 105
- The Proper Watering Technique 106
  - How & When to Water 106
- Fertilization 107
  - Types of Fertilizers: 107
  - Frequency of Fertilization 108
  - Amount of Fertilizer 108

Seeds or Cuttings? 109
- Starting from Seeds: Pros and Cons 109
  - Instructions for Starting from Seeds 110
  - Best Time of Year for Starting from Seeds 110
- Starting from Cuttings: Pros and Cons 111
  - Instructions for Starting from Cuttings 112
  - Best Time of Year for Starting from Cuttings 112

Troubleshooting & Problem-Solving 113
- Problem #1: Getting plants that are not suitable for your space 113
- Problem #2: Giving too much care to your veggies 113
- Problem #3: Improper watering 114
- Problem #4: Too low moisture 114
- Problem #5: Improper use of pots 114

Conclusion 115

BOOK 4: Seasonal Gardening 117

Introduction 119

Understanding the Growing Seasons in Your Area 120
- Growing Season Map 120
- Zone Map 120
- How to Use Them Together 120

- Choosing the Right Crops for Each Season 121
  - *Spring Crops* *121*
  - *Summer Crops* *121*
  - *Fall Crops* *121*
  - *Winter Crops* *122*

Succession Planting 123
- Techniques 123
- Timing 123

How to Preserve Your Harvest 124
- Canning 124
- Freezing 124
- Drying 124
- Fermenting 125
- Tips For Maximizing Your Reserves 125

Preparing for the Next Season 126
- Fall Cleanup 126
- Soil Amendment 126

Conclusion 127

BOOK 5: Gardening Hacks 129

Introduction 131

Maximizing Small Spaces & Productivity 132

Money-Saving Tips 133
- Regrowing Veggies From Kitchen Scraps 133
- Top 10 Money Saving Crops 135
- Plant Propagation 136
  - *Cuttings* *136*
  - *Division* *137*
  - *Layering* *137*

Growing & Harvesting Tips 139
- Fast-Growing Vegetables 139
- Growing Berries In Containers 140
  - *How to Grow Blueberries* *141*
- The 4 Best Perennial Vegetables 143
- Growing Vegetables In A Bottle 144

Essential Things to Think About..*144*

Step-by-Step Process..*145*

Conclusion 147

BONUS: Electroculture 148

Introduction 148

Basic Principles of Electroculture 149

Electroculture Techniques for Vegetable Gardening 150

Electrostatic Field Application 150

Soil Electrical Conductivity Management..150

Plasma Agriculture 151

Seed Treatment with Electromagnetic Fields 151

Magnetized Water Irrigation 152

Equipment and Setup for Home Gardeners 153

Necessary Equipment 153

Setting Up and Maintaining Equipment 153

Safety Precautions and Best Practices 154

Equipment Storage and Care 154

Applications in Vegetable Gardening 155

Challenges and Limitations for Home Gardeners 156

Energy Consumption 156

Infrastructure Requirements 156

Potential Negative Effects on the Environment 156

Potential Negative Effects on Human Health...156

Learning Curve and Technical Expertise 157

Conclusion 158

FOREWORD

Vegetable gardening is a magical and transformative experience, where the soil meets the seed, the sun meets the rain and the result is a beautiful and bountiful harvest of fresh, wholesome, and nutritious produce. Gardening has been a beloved pastime for centuries, offering a unique opportunity to nurture, grow and harvest our own food, connect with nature and create a sense of peace and fulfillment in our lives. It is a journey of growth and discovery, a celebration of life, and a reconnection with nature. Whether you are a seasoned gardener, a curious hobbyist, or a complete beginner, this comprehensive guide will inspire you, inform you, and guide you as you embark on your own journey of vegetable gardening. And, what better way to start than by growing your own fresh, wholesome and delicious vegetables in your own backyard or balcony? This comprehensive guide is designed especially for beginners and will take you on a journey of discovery, exploring the exciting and rewarding world of vegetable gardening.

From selecting the right location and preparing the soil, to choosing the right seeds and plants, and understanding the basics of water, sunlight, and nutrition, this guide will provide you with a comprehensive and thorough foundation for your vegetable gardening journey. With step-by-step instructions and helpful tips, you will learn how to create and maintain a thriving vegetable garden, regardless of your experience, the size of your plot, or the climate you live in.

Not only will you enjoy the fresh and delicious produce from your garden, but you will also experience the satisfaction of nurturing and caring for your plants, the joy of watching them grow, and the peace of mind that comes from knowing where your food comes from. With this guide as your companion, you will embark on a journey of growth, discovery, and fulfillment, and discover the magic of vegetable gardening. So, let's get started!

Have a good read,

Melanie J. Davis

BOOK 1:

Vegetable Gardening Basic

Introduction

Vegetable gardening is an enjoyable and rewarding activity that provides us with a fresh and nutritious source of food. It's a wonderful way to connect with nature, cultivate a green thumb, and get outside in the sunshine. Whether you are a beginner or an experienced gardener, the basics of vegetable gardening are easy to learn and provide a foundation for a lifetime of gardening success. In this chapter, we will cover the essentials of vegetable gardening, including soil preparation, seed selection, planting techniques, and ongoing care. By following these simple guidelines, you can grow an abundant and delicious vegetable garden in your own backyard. So grab your gloves, grab your trowel, and let's get started!

How to Plan Your Vegetable Garden

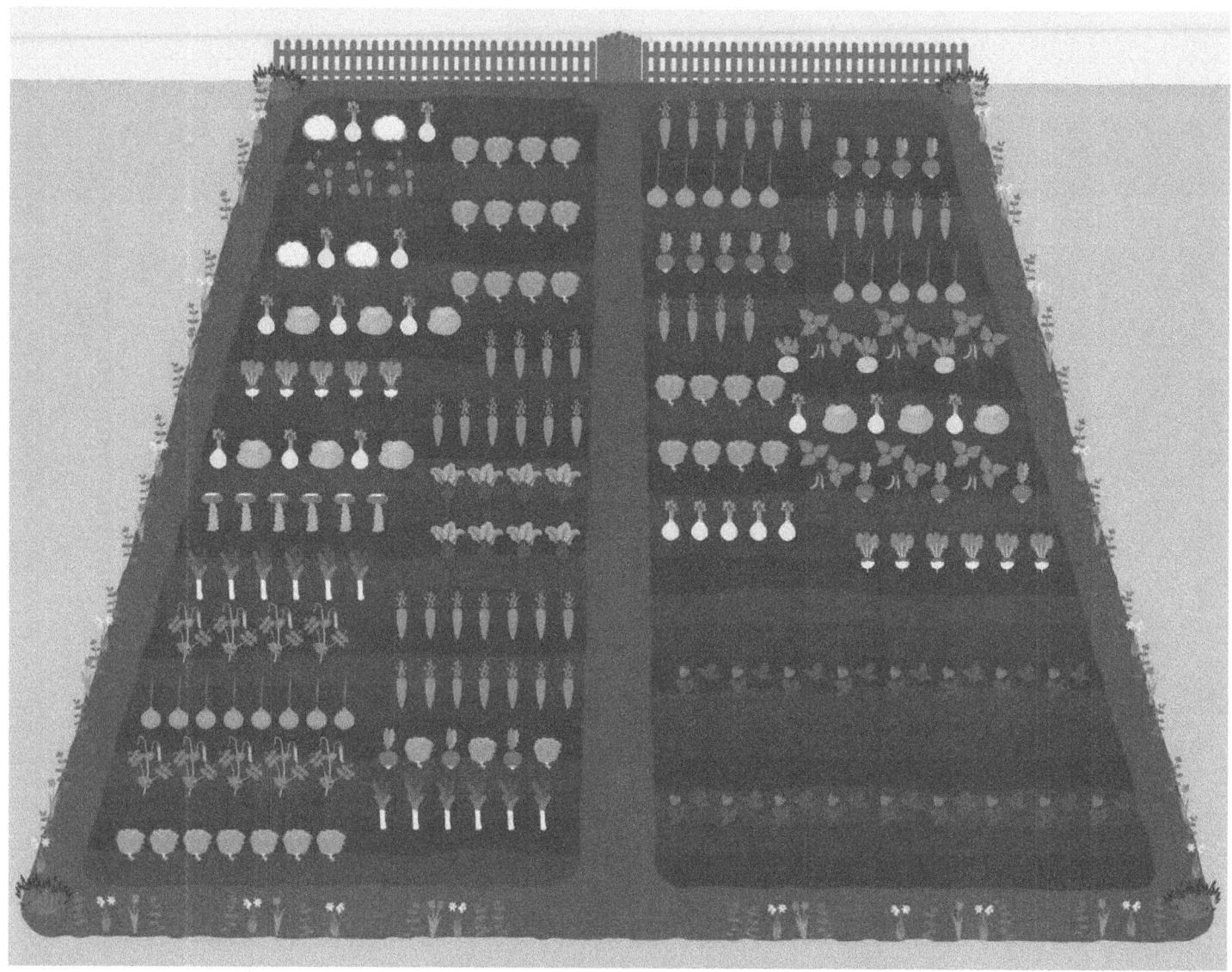

Having a green space at home is definitely a blessing. If plants are your passion and you love to grow fruits and vegetables, you may consider dedicating a corner of your garden to a small vegetable garden that allows you to have healthy, 0-mile produce right at home. Dedicating a piece of the garden to vegetables is not difficult. Let's see how to plan and implement a home vegetable garden.

Location, size and orientation

Having a vegetable garden in your backyard depends on the size of your outdoor space. In general, if you have a very large space you can set aside about 10 square meters for cultivation. As for the choice of location, much depends on what you want to grow, but in any case it is essential to have a flat, drained soil rich in organic substances that will ensure the growth of healthy and lush vegetables. It is best to choose a very sunny area because vegetables usually need several hours of direct sunlight.

The location and orientation of the vegetable garden are two very important features for successful cultivation. These preliminary choices directly affect the yield of vegetables because they determine how much light the plants will get. When planning a vegetable garden, you cannot help but consider these fundamental aspects, and if you do not know where to start, here are some tips that will come in handy.

What is the best location? - The first question to ask yourself when you start planning your vegetable garden is "what is the best location?" Certainly, the closer it is to your home, the less time it will take you to get there. This is no small consideration since in most cases the vegetable garden will be a passion for tending to almost every day, especially in summer when you will have to water. That is why it is recommended to place the vegetable garden near any source of water, as you well know plants cannot do without it.

After defining the most suitable areas, consider the presence of possible obstacles, such as trees, hedges and buildings, which could shade the crops. Having avoided the shady areas, it is time to make the final decision and start working the soil for the vegetable garden in a full sun position to ensure the plants get the light they need to photosynthesize and, consequently, be productive.

How to orient the garden? - After considering the most attractive areas in which to place the vegetable garden, you will need to decide on the orientation of the cultivated beds. Orienting a vegetable garden means designing it so that the longest side of the cultivated area is laid out along a given Cartesian axis. The best exposure for a vegetable garden is along the north-south axis because this increases the availability of light for the plants, which, placed in rows parallel to this axis, will not suffer from their own shade as the sun turns.

Some vegetable gardens will have to be placed in environments that are not entirely suitable, such as, for example, those grown in small urban gardens placed on the side of houses. In such situations, or if you grow in pots placed on balconies, you will need to orient the vegetable garden toward the south or, alternatively, toward the southeast or southwest, again to ensure that the plants get as much sun as possible. Avoid north-facing placements; in these positions vegetables receive so little light that it will be difficult to expect abundant and healthy harvests, not to mention that you will have to work hard to get them to produce.

Structure and fencing

Making a vegetable garden is a fun experience, but at the same time it takes time and effort, so protecting it is essential. This should be done especially if we have children in the house or pets such as dogs and cats that will certainly not miss an opportunity to explore. To secure the vegetables, it is a good idea to create a fence with iron stakes spaced about a meter apart and complement them with a wire mesh that is high enough, but with a small gap for passage. The arrangement of plants within the vegetable garden also plays an important role; they should be arranged in an orderly manner so that they grow in the best way possible. In addition, they should be arranged in aligned rows creating a small corridor in which to pass and move freely.

How to prepare your soil

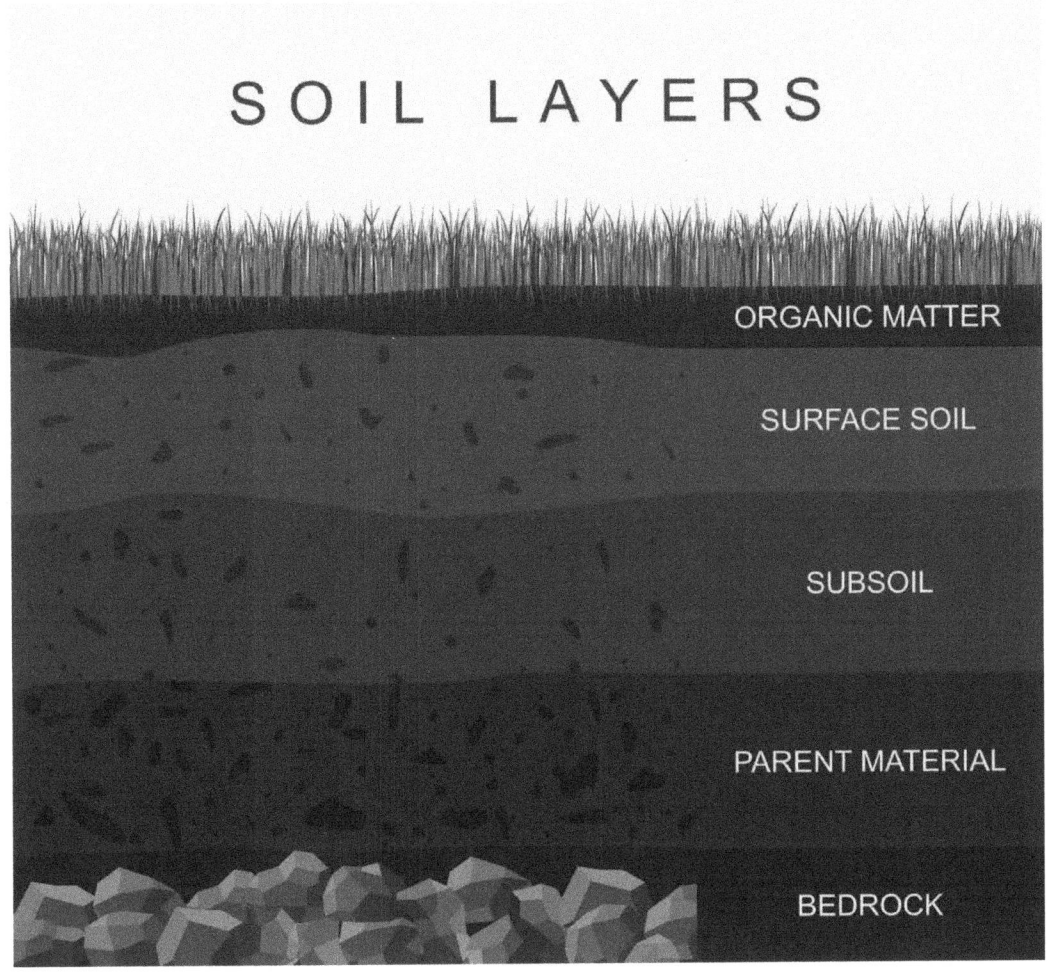

To successfully create a lush and fruitful garden, you must understand how to prepare the soil for it. The final outcome of your cultivation will be greatly influenced by how well the soil is prepared for the various crops. This is because it is crucial that the soil be prepared to support the plants you choose to plant. The importance of soil maintenance will be explained in more depth in the lines that follow, along with the steps you must do before you can start planting in your garden. Working the soil and doing quality background fertilization are two essential components of any farmer's job, even the most novice. In fact, the soil will reap many benefits, such as:

- Increased fertility
- A softer texture
- Easily penetrable for plant roots
- A greater ability to retain moisture at the same time avoiding waterlogging

In short, you will necessarily have to start with taking care of your soil. Let's see how.

When to prepare the soil?

Let's assume that you can start your vegetable garden at any time of the year, but of course some months are better than others:

- For planting we recommend you wait until march
- For transplanting already formed seedlings, on the other hand, we advise you to wait for the months of april and may

The best time of year is in the spring. Your crops will be able to benefit fully from the summer heat in this way. Additionally, we advise not working the soil immediately following or during a drought. In the first scenario, the soil will really be heavier than usual and the clods won't break down adequately; in the second scenario, however, the soil will be too hard. So when can you start tending the vegetable garden? When the soil is damp enough to make the clouds crumble and when the soil is in a moderate climate.

First step to prepare the soil

Here's a methodical piece of advice: If you're untrained, don't spend too much time hoeing and digging each day. Gardening vegetables needs patience and persistence; it is preferable to accomplish a little each day rather than a lot at first and then struggle to maintain the pace. You will also need to equip yourself with a variety of tools:

- Work gloves
- Pickaxe
- Rake
- Spade
- Shovel

Once you have these first, fundamental tools, you must begin clearing the area of any weeds or shrubs, being careful to cut them out at the root to stop them from sprouting again. This first cleanup will consist of several steps:

- Mowing the grass, using a mowing bar or a more convenient brush cutter
- A shallow hoeing aimed at removing turf roots
- You will also need to remove larger, bulky stones and rocks, the presence of which could prevent new crops from taking root as well as possible

You could even send a sample of your soil to a qualified farmer for analysis if you're determined to get it correctly. The ideal ratio of clay, sand, and soil is required for a vegetable garden to thrive. Once all of these fundamental tasks have been completed, you can begin to focus on the specifics of preparing your vegetable garden by spading. With careful and effective spading, your soil will gain looseness and permeability, among other advantages. So all you have to do is use a spade or pitchfork and insert it into the soil to a depth of about 12 inches, then pry it up with the handle. Next, you can choose between two different methods depending on how you intend to cultivate your soil:

- If you want to engage in organic cultivation, then you will simply split the top crust, thus dividing the underground roots

- If you do not want to devote yourself to organic cultivation, you can turn over all the soil devoted to the vegetable garden clod by clod

This distinction results from the presence of a variety of microorganisms, even deep inside the soil, which, if exposed to light, could perish and reduce the soil's fertility. To keep the soil as rich and fruitful as possible, organic farming is starting to abandon the practice of spading the soil with turned clods.

In any case, we advise that you proceed with traditional spading anyway: turn the clods over and be vigorous, giving the soil the right sprint to tackle whatever type of cultivation you decide to undertake next, especially if your soil has never been spaded before and if the roots of plants and shrubs are unquestionably bulky.

Basic fertilization

Because your soil needs to be enhanced, background fertilizing after spading is crucial. By doing this, you will give the soil all the nutrients it requires, soften it, and increase its capacity to hold moisture. These are the fertilizers that may be most useful to you for this purpose:

- Horse Manure
- Cow Manure
- Chicken Manure
- Compost
- Humus

Regarding quantities, we recommend that you use 4kg of manure per square meter for background fertilization.

Milling

The soil is now ready for milling, but first you must break up the massive clods that are spading left behind. To accomplish this, you'll need a pick or a hoe to break up the dirt and combine it with the compost. The next step is to use a rake to level up the soil's surface as much as you can so that you don't leave any harmful slopes or small holes in the soil that could cause your crops to stagnate. Lastly, be sure to pick up any final weeds or stones. After completing all of this, give your vegetable garden a rest and wait until the soil and compost are thoroughly blended. You will then be prepared to plant what you want most. Always keep in mind that great yields begin with good and attentive vegetable garden maintenance. Avoid being caught off guard!

How many and what are the soil types?

We said that knowing the type of soil is crucial in deciding which plants to grow because, over time, different plant species have adapted to grow in soils with certain characteristics. In nature we can find 6 different types of soil:

- Gravelly
- Sandy
- Silty
- Clayey
- Calcareous
- Medium-textured.

Gravel soil: not very suitable for vegetable garden plants - Gravelly soil contains at least 40 percent stones, crushed stones and coarse sands. It is a very porous soil, where water flows quickly, dry and poor in organic matter and therefore not very fertile. If you have this type of soil you will have to work as much as possible with a spade and hoe to remove stones and pebbles and add sand and manure.

Sandy soil: fertilize and water often - Sandy soil is at least 70% sand. It is light, loose, very permeable and low in organic matter. If you crush a handful of soil from your vegetable garden and it falls apart very quickly, it means your soil is sandy. This type of soil has the advantage of being very easy to work with and, because of its light texture, contains a lot of oxygen, a valuable ally of vegetables. On the other hand, a sandy soil dries out very quickly so, especially during hotter periods, it is at greater risk of drought and you will need to irrigate more frequently.

To cultivate this type of soil you will have to frequently resort to fertilizing with manure, compost, manure and organic fertilizers. The main varieties of vegetable plants that you can grow in sandy soil, adopting appropriate improvements, in this type of soil are: garlic, onion, bell pepper, shallot, tomato, eggplant, carrot, watermelon, potato, fennel and fava bean.

Silty soil: add organic matter - Silty soil gets its name from silt, a very fertile, grainy mud of which it is at least 50 percent. Since ancient Egyptian times, silt has been recognized for its fertilizing properties but, if in excess, it makes the soil compact and difficult to work. The granules, enveloping the roots, make it difficult for them to breathe and can cause waterlogging.

This type of soil leaves a whitish residue on the hands similar to talcum powder, and in the case of heavy summer storms, when it can get wet and dry quickly, it tends to form a surface crust. So silty soil is therefore suitable for growing vegetable plants as long as you add the organic matter and-if necessary-sand, which makes its structure more suitable for tilling. The varieties that are best adapted to this type of soil are: chicory, radicchio, beets and broad beans.

Limestone soil: ideal for cabbages and cauliflowers - Limestone soil contains at least 20 percent limestone, making it rather white, loose and dusty and unsuitable for retaining organic matter. It is a hostile soil for growing a vegetable garden because, having a very basic ph it is unsuitable for most vegetable plants that prefer acid or neutral PH. If your soil is very light and when it rains it compacts, it is probably limestone.

At this point you can intervene by incorporating manure to make the ph more acidic and to provide the plants with the organic matter that this soil is poor in, and peat loam to have the right consistency for working. In the case of particularly compacted soil, we recommend that you also add sand. A limey soil is ideal for cabbages and cauliflowers that fear an acid ph and for aromatic vegetable garden seedlings such as thyme and rosemary. If the soil is not too dry, green light is also given to melons, leeks and artichokes.

Appropriately enriched with organic matter, a lime-type soil will also usefully accommodate garlic, carrots, beets, radishes, parsnips, beans, peas, lentils, beans, tomatoes, lettuce and Jerusalem artichokes.

Clay soil: how to make it better - Clay soil is probably one of the least suitable for growing vegetable garden plants. So if you are faced with this type of soil, you will face a few more obstacles. If the clods in your vegetable garden are very difficult to break, contain few roots and insects, and in dry periods the soil surface cracks, arm yourself with patience and goodwill because you will have to deal with hostile clay soil. This type of soil, while rich in nutrients, is heavy and suffocates plant roots in addition to retaining water causing insidious waterlogging.

The good news is that even clay soil can be improved. Add organic materials such as manure, all-purpose organic soil, peat, compost, as well as inorganic materials such as sand (preferably mixed with gravel), ash and agricultural chalk to your soil. You will need to bury these materials not too deeply, after digging up the soil. Ask your local dealer for advice on choosing the right products and how to incorporate them into your soil. As for which varieties to grow, clay soil is similar to loam soil but, once worked as described above, you can enrich your garden with wide other varieties.

Medium-textured soil: the best type for vegetable garden plants - As the name implies, medium-textured soil has intermediate characteristics where, unlike the other types, all the components are present within it (about 50-70 percent sand, 25-40 percent silt, 5-15 percent clay, and 2 percent humus). This type of soil, usually of alluvial origin, is the most common and the best to host vegetable garden seedlings. In this case, what you will need to consider when choosing your crops are the characteristics of your climate zone.

Medium-textured soil is able to retain moisture while avoiding waterlogging and is rich in organic matter and nutrients. Because it is soft, the roots can sink in and do not run the risk of being smothered, as is the case with clay soil, in case of rain. If your soil is soft, moist and clods break easily between your fingers, it is medium-textured. The important thing will be to fertilize it periodically and to resort to mulching to protect the plants from weeds and to maintain the right temperature of the topmost part of the roots.

Choosing & Starting Seeds

In this section, we will cover all the important aspects of selecting and starting seeds for your garden. You will learn about the methods for starting them, and how to care for your seedlings to ensure their healthy growth. We will also touch upon the process of saving your own seeds from your garden, so that you can have a sustainable source of plants year after year. By the end of this chapter, you will have a comprehensive understanding of the seed-starting process and be well on your way to a thriving and productive vegetable garden.

SEED SELECTION

The process of starting a vegetable garden can be fun and rewarding, but one of the most crucial tasks is selecting the proper seeds. Your garden's success or failure can be largely attributed to the seeds you choose, so take care when doing so. Here is a comprehensive checklist to help you select the best seeds for your vegetable garden.

- Consider your climate and growing conditions: Different vegetable plants have varying requirements for temperature, light, and moisture, so it's crucial to choose seeds that will grow well in your area. Make sure to research the average temperature and rainfall for your region and select seeds that are suited for these conditions.

- Determine the right time to plant: The timing of planting is also crucial to the success of your garden. Make sure to choose seeds that can be planted at the right time for your climate. For example, cool-season crops like lettuce, spinach, and peas should be planted in early spring, while warm-season crops like tomatoes, peppers, and eggplants should be planted in late spring or early summer.

- Select seeds based on maturity time: Consider the amount of time you have to devote to your garden and choose seeds that mature within that time frame. For example, if you only have a few months to devote to your garden, you might want to choose quick-maturing crops like radishes or bush beans.

- Choose seeds based on taste and nutritional value: When selecting seeds, think about the taste and nutritional value of the resulting produce. If you're growing vegetables for a family, choose seeds that will produce crops with the best taste and highest nutritional value.

- Buy seeds from reputable sources: Make sure to buy seeds from reputable seed companies or nurseries. These companies generally sell high-quality seeds that are tested for germination rates and disease resistance.

- Look for disease-resistant seeds: Choose seeds that are resistant to common diseases in your area. This will help ensure that your crops are healthy and productive.

- Consider the size of your garden: The size of your garden will determine how many seeds you need. Make sure to choose seeds that will fit in your garden and not take over.

Seed Starting Methods

Starting seeds is an important step in growing a successful vegetable garden. It allows you to grow plants from the earliest stages, increasing your chances of having strong, healthy, and productive plants. In this chapter, we will cover various methods for starting seeds, including indoor and outdoor seed starting. Before delving into the core of this paragraph, it is good to keep in mind some preliminary considerations that apply regardless of the type of technique you intend to use.

- Keep the soil moist but not waterlogged. Seeds need moisture to germinate, but too much water can cause mold and disease.
- Provide adequate light. Most seedlings need at least six hours of direct sunlight per day, or grow lights if started indoors.
- Keep the temperature consistent. Most seeds need to be kept at a temperature of around 70°F to germinate and grow.
- Provide adequate ventilation. Seedlings need fresh air to grow healthy and strong.
- Fertilize regularly. Seedlings need nutrients to grow, so make sure to fertilize them regularly with a balanced fertilizer.

Below are listed the best seed-starting techniques that you can employ depending on your needs:

1. **Indoor seed starting:** This is a popular method for starting seeds in areas with a short growing season or limited outdoor space. Indoor seed starting allows you to start seeds early and provide them with optimal growing conditions until they are ready to be planted outside. To start seeds indoors, you will need containers, soil, and grow lights.

2. **Soil blocking:** This method involves using a soil blocker to make compact blocks of soil that contain the seeds. Soil blocks provide an ideal growing environment for seeds, allowing them to grow roots quickly and avoiding the need to transplant seedlings.

3. **Peat pots:** Peat pots are made from compressed peat moss and are biodegradable. They can be planted directly in the garden, avoiding the stress of transplanting seedlings. Peat pots are also environmentally friendly, as they break down in the soil over time.

4. **Cell packs:** Cell packs are plastic trays with individual cells for each seed. They are a convenient and inexpensive way to start seeds, and the cells help prevent overcrowding and root damage.

5. **Outdoor seed starting:** This method involves directly planting seeds in the garden. Outdoor seed starting is a cost-effective and straightforward option, but it requires proper timing and soil preparation. It is best for warm-season crops that can tolerate outdoor conditions.

In conclusion, seed starting is a crucial step in growing a successful vegetable garden. Whether you choose indoor or outdoor seed starting, it's important to provide your seedlings with the proper conditions to grow healthy and strong. By following these tips and selecting the right seed-starting method for your needs, you can grow a thriving vegetable garden.

How to Collect & Store Seeds

If you want to make your vegetable garden, vegetable patch, or terrace more than simply a hobby, learning how to get and store seeds of your favorite veggies is a crucial first step. I'll explain how to collect seeds, store them, and then prepare them for planting the next year in the following few lines. You'll be able to continue growing your preferred crops this way without needing to visit a professional nursery every year.

We have said that storing seeds is critical to jumpstarting your favorite crops. But let's start with the basics: *what is a seed?* It is nothing more than an egg cell transformed by the fertilization process. In short, the seed is the organ responsible for plant dissemination. Seeds are also low in water, which is why they can boast a long shelf life. The seeds you are going to collect and store must have specific characteristics. They will therefore have to be:

- Obtained by open pollination
- Ripe
- Healthy
- With good color
- Without roughness

How to harvest seeds from your garden

Although all plants have their own characteristics and should therefore be treated differently, there are still some general rules that apply to your vegetable garden.

First, it is important that you pay close attention to the growth process of your plants. You will need to select the best, strongest, hardiest plants that best resist disease and climate change. Avoid the last fruits or flowers of the season, which are now weakened. As already mentioned, we recommend that you prefer seeds from open pollination-this way you will be able to get plants that are very similar to those from which the seeds were taken. If, on the contrary, you should take seeds from hybrid plants, expect plants that will not retain the previous characteristics and will give rise to cross-pollination.

When to collect seeds?

Especially for vegetables, we recommend that you wait for warm, dry weather. Once the right season arrives, the best time will be around 10 a.m., when the dew will have completely evaporated by then. To be sure that the seed has reached maturity, you can observe the flowers or fruits: the flowers should be dry, while the fruits should be well ripe. Only at this point will your seeds have taken up all the nutrients they need to support the germination process ahead. Remember: only a mature seed will guarantee you beautiful sprouts.

The last important tip to follow at this stage of harvesting is to collect more seeds per plant. Doing so will give you a better chance of having a good seedling.

How to Store Seeds

To have good planting and, consequently, good production, you will have to make sure you store them as well as possible. Here are my tips:

- Store the seeds in paper bags and not plastic; the latter, in fact, do not facilitate transpiration and could cause mold inside. In any case, the envelopes or containers should not be sealed and should be completely dry;
- Always label all your seeds so that there is no confusion when planting: Note the name of the plant, the date of harvest, and any other notes
- Let the seeds dry in a cool, ventilated place;
- After the drying phase, you can store the seeds in a cellar, but one that maintains a temperature between 41F° and 50°F and is not humid;
- Periodically check your seeds and remove any that are rotten or moldy;

The best way to store seeds is to place them in airtight glass containers, which should be stored in a cool, dry and dark place. With these precautions, tomato seeds will retain their germination capacity for 4 years, melon and bell pepper seeds for 5 years, and zucchini even for 10. The only exception is eggplant seeds, stored in the refrigerator at temperatures around 41.0 °F (5 °C), which will retain their viability for about 5 years.

SOIL TEMPERATURE AND SEED GERMINATION CHART

F°	32°	41°	50°	59°	68°	77°	86°	95°	104°
parsnips	172	57	27	20	14	15	32		
onion	136	50	13	7	5	4	4	13	
spinach	62	23	12	7	6	5	6		
lettuce	49	15	7	4	3	2	3		
cabbage		51	17	10	7	6	6	9	
carrots		50	17	10	7	6	6	9	
celery		41	16	12	7				
peas		46	14	9	8	6	6		
radishes		29	11	6	4	4	4	3	
asparagus			52	24	14	10	11	19	28
tomatoes			43	14	8	6	6	9	
parsley			29	17	14	13	13		
sweet corn			21	12	7	4	4	3	
cauliflower			119	9	6	5	5		
beets			14	9	6	5	6		
turnips			5	3	2	1	1	1	3
lima beans				30	17	6	7		
okra				27	17	12	7	6	7
peppers				25	13	8	8	9	
snap beans				16	11	8	6	6	
cucumbers				13	6	4	3	5	
squash					6	4	3		
eggplant					13	8	5		

Understanding Basic Plant Biology

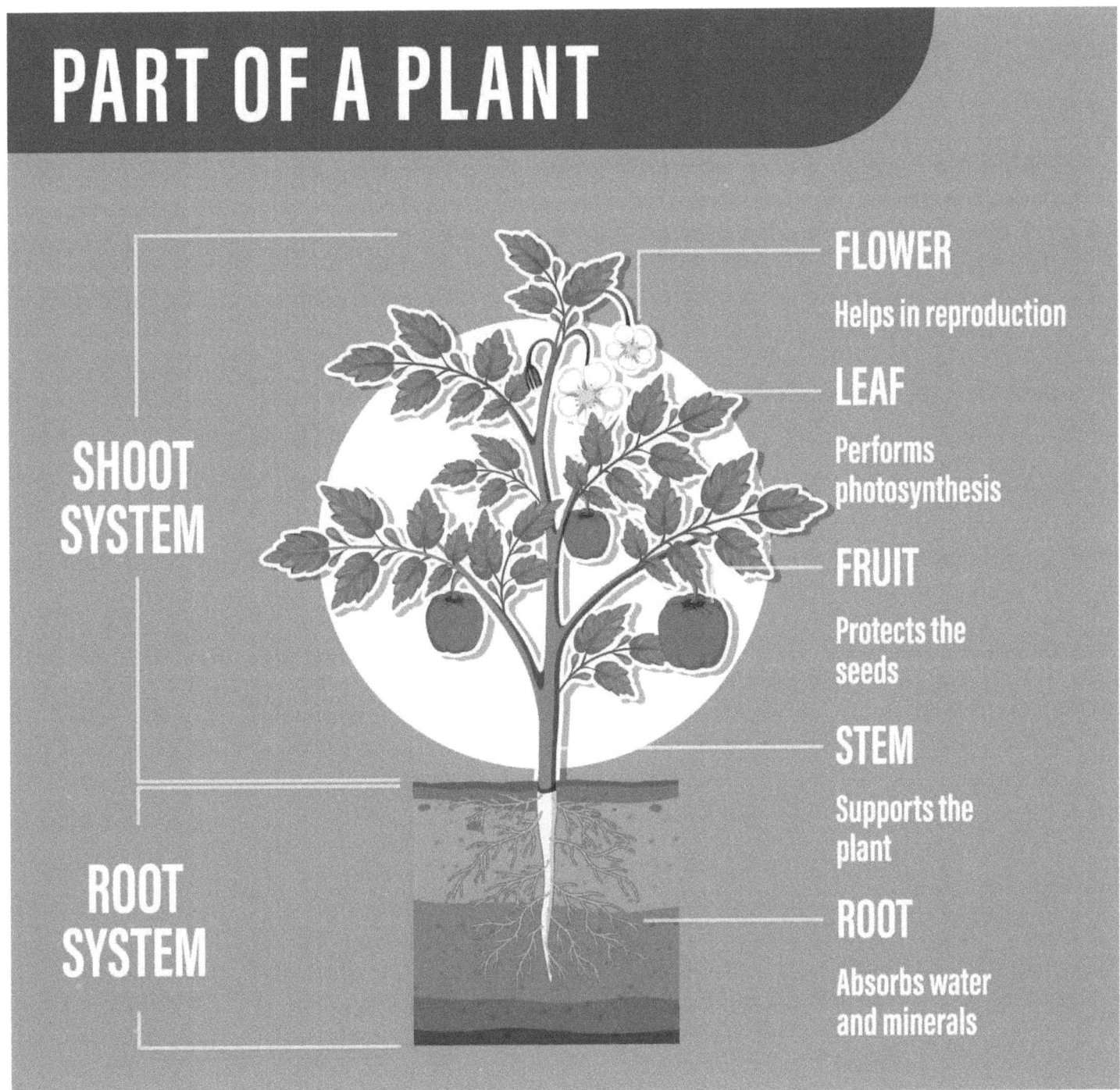

Knowing the parts of the plant is essential to proceed with its classification. Indeed, distinguishing its various elements, their arrangement, absence or form, allows us to know the anatomical coordinates of our plant. There are 6 main plant parts: root, stem, leaf, flower, inflorescence, and fruit. The three main organs are root, stem and leaf, which mainly have the functions of nutrition. In contrast, reproductive functions are related to flower, fruit and seed.

1) The root - The root is the underground part of a plant. It not only supports the plant, anchoring it to the soil, but also provides water and mineral elements, absorbing them from the earth. It also often stores them as a reserve. In some cases, the root constitutes the active part of the medicinal plant, while in others it is the most toxic and harmful element.

2) The stem - The stem is the support of the leaves and encloses the conducting vessels. It is the transit channel through which the nymph rises up toward the leaves and descends true to the root. It may be aerial or subterranean.

3) The leaf - The leaf is a basic organ of plants and is generally green. Its main function is to fix carbon and expel excess water, through transpiration. There is also chlorophyll on the leaves, which is essential for chlorophyll photosynthesis, a process that can give nutrition to the plant.

4) The flower - The flower is a highly specialized bud. Of all plant parts, it is the sexed organ, sometimes the only one capable of ensuring reproduction and perpetuation of the species. The complete anatomy of a flower includes the presence of a calyx, a corolla, stamens and a pistil. If even one of these elements is missing, its morphology is said to be incomplete. The peduncle is the support of the flower, at the base of which is a small leaf called a bract. The flowers may be solitary or united in inflorescences of various shapes.

5) The inflorescence - This term refers to a grouping of flowers supported by a single stalk.

6) The fruit - The fruit is the final maturation of a fertilized ovary. It contains the ovules, which are transformed into seeds. The seeds can be planted and thus germinate a new plant, belonging to the same species. Fruits can be divided into two categories: dry fruits and fleshy fruits.

How do plants thrive?

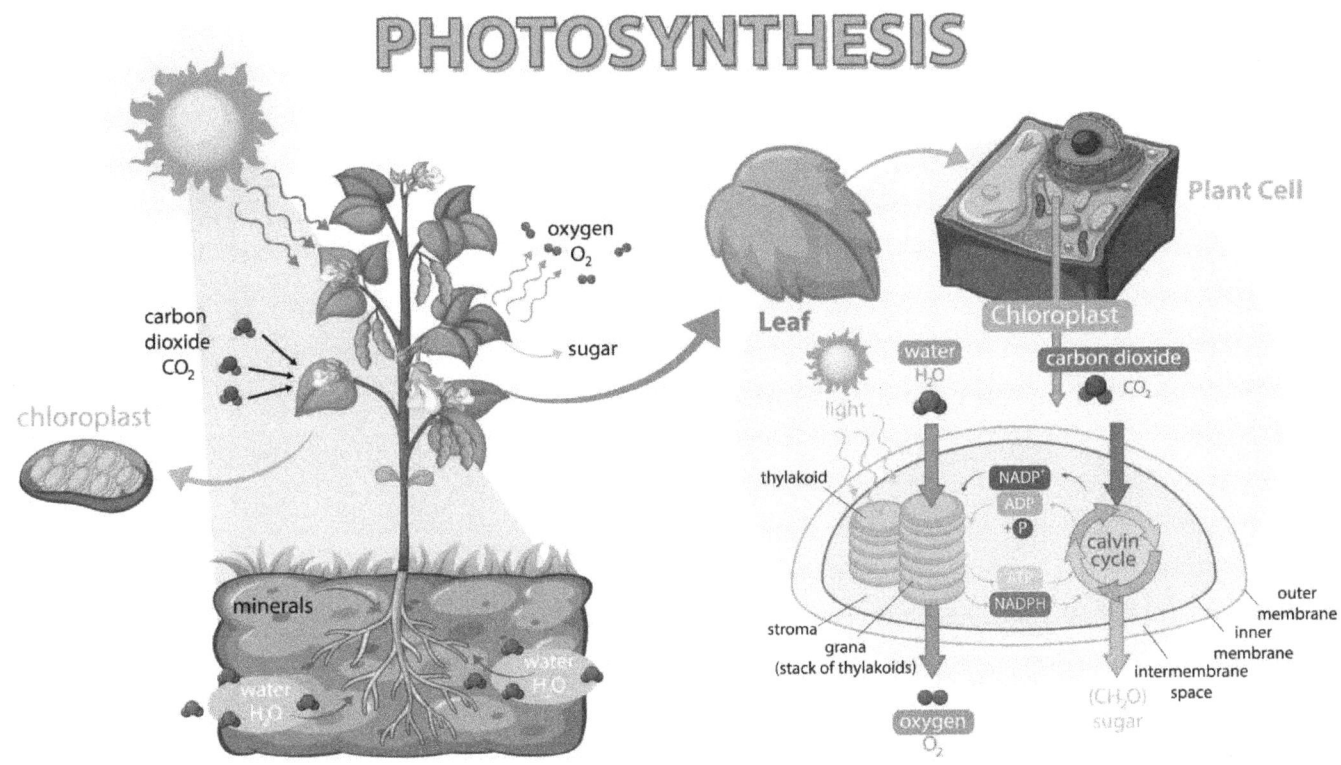

Plants are living things, which is one of the reasons they are so interesting to care for and collect. We can easily guess what another living being requires to survive based on our personal experience: food, oxygen, water, and rest. As a result, learning how to care for an animal is relatively simple. Plants, on the other hand, are a different story because, while they are alive and require care, they are very different from ours. That is why understanding their processes and requirements is the most important key to ensuring that your green companions grow healthy, radiant, and strong.

Humans require organic substances to obtain the nutrients they require, but plants are autotrophic beings. In other words, they make their own food from inorganic materials. Plants require inorganic compounds such as phosphorus, calcium, nitrogen, magnesium, and other mineral salts to be self-sufficient. These nutrients come from water and soil. A plant requires four basic things to survive: water, soil or substrate, air, and sunlight. It can generate everything it requires from these things.

The feeding process of the plant consists of three steps: taking nutrients from the substrate and air, converting these nutrients into food, and transporting the food throughout the plant. It obtains the food it requires to continue growing and performing its vital functions through this process. Another significant difference between plant and human diets is that we gain weight, whereas in plants, the portion of the food that is not used/consumed immediately is stored in leaves, roots, seeds, and fruits.

Step-by-step nurture process

When you water the plant, the process begins. Inorganic compounds in the substrate are dissolved by the water, making them more available to the plant. The plant's root hairs collect nutrients and mineral salts, combining them to form raw sap. The sap rises through the woody vessels, which are very tiny tubes that run through the plant like veins and arteries.

Stomata are tiny pores on the plant's leaves. Carbon dioxide enters through the stomata, combines with the raw sap, and initiates photosynthesis, which produces converted sap and oxygen.

Photosynthesis requires sunlight, which is caught by chlorophyll, a material in plant leaves that gives plants their distinctive green hue, in the same way that the concentration of melanin in human skin gives color to the skin. The plant produces oxygen as a byproduct of the photosynthesis process, which people utilize to breathe. This is why forests and woodlands are sometimes referred to as "plant lungs," as they produce the oxygen we breathe. Once photosynthetic sap is formed in the leaves, it is transmitted throughout the plant via the liberian vessels, feeding all parts of the plant, including the woody stems.

What about the fertilizer?

Fertilization is the process of introducing elements into the soil that can increase its fertility. So improving the performance of our crops is a good activity. Since the nutrient supply is constrained and prone to depletion in the case of potted crops, this is essential to the cultivation's success because, unlike in a garden, a plant cannot use its roots to probe deeply for nutrients. However, fertilization is still necessary for open field cultivation, for instance, to restore the fertility of severely used soils.

The most significant factor is that healthy plants are better able to withstand disease. Low yields, stunted growth, and leaf chlorosis are all signs of a nitrogen-deficient plant. On the other hand, too much nitrogen disrupts the biological cycle, making the plant an accessible target for insect attack. There are many different fertilizer products that may be used for gardens and crops, and each one has unique properties that cater to different plant demands.

What do fertilizers contain? There are 12 elements that are essential for plant growth and production. We can summarize them into three categories:

- **Macroelements:** Nitrogen (N), Phosphorus (P) and Potassium (K),
- **Mesoelements:** Calcium, Sulfur, Magnesium, Iron,

- **Microelements:** Boron, Zinc, Manganese, Molybdenum, Copper.

Because plants have different needs, there are products designed for specific uses, with different contents of the various elements. These are clearly indicated on the package, in what is called a title. The title of fertilizer indicates what and how many nutrients are contained, expressed as a percentage by mass.

The three primary macronutrients required by plants are nitrogen (N), phosphorus (P), and potassium (K), and these elements are usually represented by their chemical symbols in a fertilizer ratio. The ratio is expressed as three numbers, such as 10-10-10, indicating the percentage of each nutrient contained in the fertilizer. Fertilizer ratios can vary greatly depending on the type of plant and its specific nutrient requirements. For example, a fertilizer with a high ratio of nitrogen, such as 20-5-5, would be best for promoting leafy green growth in plants, while a fertilizer with a higher ratio of phosphorus, such as 10-20-10, would be best for promoting flower and fruit production.

Fertilizer Ratios for Common Vegetables

The right fertilizer will provide your plants with the nutrients they need to grow strong and produce high-quality products. However, choosing the right fertilizer can be challenging, as different vegetables have different nutrient requirements. In this chapter, we will discuss the most suitable fertilizer ratios for the most common vegetables.

- Tomatoes: Tomatoes are heavy feeders and need a lot of nitrogen to produce lush foliage and fruit. A fertilizer ratio of 5-10-10 (nitrogen-phosphorus-potassium) is ideal for tomatoes.

- Carrots: Carrots require a low level of nitrogen and high levels of phosphorus and potassium to produce strong roots. A fertilizer ratio of 3-10-3 is ideal for carrots.

- Cucumbers: Cucumbers are fast-growing plants that also require a lot of nitrogen for leafy growth. A fertilizer ratio of 4-6-8 is suitable for cucumbers.

- Lettuce: Lettuce is a cool-season crop that requires a low level of nitrogen and higher levels of phosphorus and potassium. A fertilizer ratio of 2-6-6 is suitable for lettuce.

- Peppers: Peppers need a balanced fertilizer with a slightly higher phosphorus content to encourage fruit production. A fertilizer ratio of 5-10-5 is ideal for peppers.

- Squash: Squash plants are heavy feeders and need a lot of nitrogen for leafy growth. A fertilizer ratio of 5-6-6 is suitable for squash.

- Beans: Beans are nitrogen-fixing plants that need a balanced fertilizer with a slightly higher level of phosphorus. A fertilizer ratio of 4-6-6 is ideal for beans.

- Peas: Peas are also nitrogen-fixing plants that need a balanced fertilizer with a slightly higher level of phosphorus. A fertilizer ratio of 4-6-6 is suitable for peas.

It's important to note that these ratios are general guidelines, and the specific fertilizer needs of your plants may vary based on soil type, climate, and other factors. Additionally, it's always best to follow the instructions on the fertilizer package and use a soil test to determine the specific needs of your garden soil.

How to Grow Common Vegetables

TOMATOES

Types of Tomatoes: There are many different varieties of tomatoes, each with its own unique characteristics. Some common types of tomatoes include cherry tomatoes, which are small and sweet; beefsteak tomatoes, which are large and meaty; and heirloom tomatoes, which are prized for their unique flavors and often used in gourmet cooking.

Growth Habits: Tomatoes are warm-season plants that prefer a warm, sunny climate and well-drained soil. They grow best in soil that has a pH between 6.0 and 7.0. Tomatoes are typically grown as annuals, but can also be grown as perennials in warm climates.

Planting: Tomatoes can be planted either from seed or from seedlings. When planting from seed, start the seeds indoors about 6 to 8 weeks before the last expected frost date. When planting seedlings, wait until the soil has warmed up and all danger of frost has passed. Plant seedlings in a sunny location and water them well after planting.

Harvesting: Tomatoes are typically ready to harvest about 70 to 80 days after planting. They should be picked when they are fully ripe, but before they become overripe. Overripe tomatoes will have a softer texture and may be more prone to decay.

Yield: The expected yield from a single tomato plant will vary depending on the variety and growing conditions, but a single plant can produce anywhere from 10 to 20 pounds of fruit.

Watering and Irrigation: Tomatoes need to be watered consistently and deeply to produce the best fruit. Water them deeply once a week, or more frequently in hot, dry conditions. Avoid getting water on the foliage, as this can lead to disease problems.

Common Problems: Two of the most common problems that affect tomato plants are blossom-end rot and tomato fruit worm. Blossom-end rot is a calcium deficiency that affects the fruit and causes the bottom of the tomato to rot. Tomato fruit worm is a pest that can damage the fruit and reduce yields. To prevent these problems, make sure to provide your plants with adequate water and nutrients, and use appropriate pest control methods.

Cucumbers

Types of Cucumbers: There are several different types of cucumbers, including English Cucumbers, which are typically used in salads and sandwiches; Gherkins, which are ideal for making pickles; and Armenian Cucumbers *(also known as Snake Cucumbers)*, which are great for grilling and pairing with fish dishes.

Growth Habits: Cucumbers are warm-season plants that prefer a warm, sunny climate and well-drained soil. They grow best in soil that has a pH between 6.0 and 7.0. Cucumbers are typically grown as annuals, but can also be grown as perennials in warm climates.

Planting: Cucumbers can be planted either from seed or from seedlings. When planting from seed, start the seeds indoors about 2 to 3 weeks before the last expected frost date. When planting seedlings, wait until the soil has warmed up and all danger of frost has passed. Plant seedlings in a sunny location and water them well after planting.

Harvesting: Cucumbers are typically ready to harvest about 50 to 60 days after planting. They should be picked when they are firm, crisp, and bright green. Overripe cucumbers will be yellow and will have a softer texture.

Yield: The expected yield from a single cucumber plant will vary depending on the variety and growing conditions, but a single plant can produce anywhere from 5 to 10 pounds of fruit.

Watering and Irrigation: Cucumbers need to be watered consistently and deeply to produce the best fruit. Water them deeply once a week, or more frequently in hot, dry conditions. Avoid getting water on the foliage, as this can lead to disease problems.

Common Problems: Two of the most common problems that affect cucumber plants are powdery mildew and cucumber beetles. Powdery mildew is a fungal disease that affects foliage and reduces yields. Cucumber beetles are pests that can damage foliage and reduce yields. To prevent these problems, make sure to provide your plants with adequate water and nutrients, and use appropriate pest control methods.

ZUCCHINI

Types of Zucchini: There are several different types of zucchini, including green zucchini, which is the most common variety; yellow zucchini, which is similar in flavor to green zucchini but has a more vibrant color; and round zucchini, which is a smaller and more compact variety.

Growth Habits: Zucchini is a warm-season vegetable that prefers a warm, sunny climate and well-drained soil. They grow best in soil that has a pH between 6.0 and 7.0. Zucchini plants can grow quickly and can become quite large, so be sure to plant them in an area with plenty of space.

Planting: Zucchini can be planted either from seed or from seedlings. When planting from seed, start the seeds indoors about 2 to 3 weeks before the last expected frost date. When planting seedlings, wait until the soil has warmed up and all danger of frost has passed. Plant seedlings in a sunny location and water them well after planting.

Harvesting: Zucchini is typically ready to harvest about 50 to 60 days after planting. They should be picked when they are firm, tender, and green. Overripe zucchini will be larger and will have a softer texture.

Yield: The expected yield from a single zucchini plant will vary depending on the variety and growing conditions, but a single plant can produce anywhere from 3 to 10 pounds of fruit.

Watering and Irrigation: Zucchini needs to be watered consistently and deeply to produce the best fruit. Water them deeply once a week, or more frequently in hot, dry conditions. Avoid getting water on the foliage, as this can lead to disease problems.

Common Problems: Two of the most common problems that affect zucchini plants are powdery mildew and squash vine borers. Powdery mildew is a fungal disease that affects foliage and reduces yields. Squash vine borers are pests that can damage the stem and reduce yields. To prevent these problems, make sure to provide your plants with adequate water and nutrients, and use appropriate pest control methods.

CAULIFLOWER

Types of Cauliflower: There are several different types of cauliflower, each with its own unique characteristics. Some of the most common types of cauliflower include:

- White Cauliflower: The most popular type of cauliflower, with a creamy white head and a mild flavor.

- Orange Cauliflower: A newer variety of cauliflower that is gaining popularity due to its bright orange color and high levels of beta-carotene.

- Purple Cauliflower: A striking variety of cauliflower with a deep purple head and a slightly nutty flavor.

Growth Habits:

Cauliflower is a cool-season crop that grows best in temperatures between 50-70°F (10-21°C). It is important to plant cauliflower in soil that is well-drained, rich in organic matter, and has a pH between 6.0-7.0. Cauliflower also requires consistent watering, as it does not tolerate drought well.

Planting:

Cauliflower can be planted in the garden in either the spring or fall, depending on the climate. In most regions, it is best to plant seeds indoors 6-8 weeks before the last expected frost. When planting, place the seeds in individual pots filled with seed-starting mix and water well. Once the seedlings are large enough to handle, transplant them into the garden about 18-24 inches apart, with 24-36 inches between rows.

Harvesting:

Cauliflower is usually ready for harvest about 75-100 days after planting, depending on the variety. To harvest, cut the head from the plant with a sharp knife, leaving a few inches of stem attached. It is important to harvest the head when it is still tight and before the buds start to open.

Expected Yield:

The yield of a cauliflower crop will depend on many factors, including the type of cauliflower, the soil conditions, and the amount of sunlight and water the plants receive. On average, a mature cauliflower plant will produce 1 head per plant (11-18oz).

Watering and Irrigation:

Cauliflower needs consistent watering, especially when the heads are forming. The soil should be kept evenly moist, but not waterlogged. A slow, deep watering once or twice a week is usually sufficient.

Common Problems:

Bolt: Cauliflower can bolt, or go to seed, if exposed to high temperatures or if the plant is stressed. To avoid bolting, be sure to plant cauliflower in soil with the correct temperature range and avoid over-fertilizing or over-watering.

Pests: Cauliflower can be susceptible to pests like aphids, flea beetles, and cabbage worms. Regularly inspecting the plants for pests and using row covers or insecticidal soap as needed can help keep these pests under control.

Lettuce

Types of Lettuce: There are many different types of lettuce, including crisphead lettuce, butterhead lettuce, and looseleaf lettuce. Some popular varieties of lettuce include Iceberg, Romaine, Buttercrunch, and Red Leaf.

Growth Habits: Lettuce is a cool-season crop that grows best in temperatures between 45 and 65°F. It prefers well-drained soil with a pH between 6.0 and 7.0. Lettuce can be grown in either full sun or partial shade, but it is important to provide adequate moisture to keep the soil evenly moist.

Planting: Lettuce can be started from seed or from seedlings. When planting from seed, start the seeds indoors about 4 to 6 weeks before the last expected frost date. When planting seedlings, wait until the soil has warmed up and all danger of frost has passed. Plant seedlings in a sunny or partially shaded location and water them well after planting.

Harvesting: Lettuce is typically ready to harvest about 40 to 50 days after planting. It can be harvested as a whole head or as individual leaves, depending on your preference. To extend the harvest season, stagger your planting so that you have a continuous supply of lettuce throughout the growing season.

Yield: The expected yield from a single lettuce plant will vary depending on the variety and growing conditions, but a single plant can produce anywhere from 2.5 to 5.5 ounces of lettuce.

Watering and Irrigation: Lettuce needs to be watered consistently and evenly to produce the best quality leaves. Water them deeply once a week, or more frequently in hot, dry conditions.

Common Problems: Two of the most common problems that affect lettuce plants are downy mildew and lettuce aphids. Downy mildew is a fungal disease that affects foliage and reduces yields. Lettuce aphids are pests that can damage the foliage and reduce yields. To prevent these problems, make sure to provide your plants with adequate water and nutrients, and use appropriate pest control methods.

Cabbage

Types of Cabbage: There are many different types of cabbage, including green cabbage, red cabbage, savoy cabbage, and Napa cabbage. Some popular varieties of cabbage include "Dynasty," "Ruby Ball," and "Savoy King."

Growth Habits: Cabbage is a cool-season crop that grows best in temperatures between 45 and 65°F. It prefers well-drained soil with a pH between 6.0 and 7.0. Cabbage can be grown in either full sun or partial shade, but it is important to provide adequate moisture to keep the soil evenly moist.

Planting: Cabbage can be started from seed or from seedlings. When planting from seed, start the seeds indoors about 4 to 6 weeks before the last expected frost date. When planting seedlings, wait until the soil has warmed up and all danger of frost has passed. Plant seedlings in a sunny or partially shaded location and water them well after planting.

Harvesting: Cabbage is ready for harvest when the heads are firm and tight. Generally, cabbage takes about 85 to 100 days from planting to harvest. Harvest the cabbage by cutting the head from the stem with a sharp knife.

Expected Yield: The yield of cabbage can vary depending on the variety and growing conditions. On average, you can expect to harvest about 4 to 10 pounds of cabbage heads.

Watering and Irrigation: Cabbage prefers evenly moist soil, but it is important not to over-water. Over-watering can lead to root rot and other problems. Water the cabbage deeply once a week or as needed to keep the soil moist.

Common Problems: Two of the most common problems when growing cabbage are clubroot and cabbage loopers. Clubroot is a soil-borne fungus that causes the roots of the cabbage plant to become stunted and distorted. To prevent clubroot, rotate your crops and avoid planting in areas where the disease has previously occurred. Cabbage loopers are the larvae of a type of moth that feed on the leaves of the cabbage plant. To prevent damage from loopers, cover the plants with a floating row cover or use an insecticide.

Carrots

Types of Carrots: Some of the most common types of carrots include: Danvers - A medium-sized, cone-shaped carrot that is popular for its sweet flavor and versatility. Nantes - A cylindrical-shaped carrot that is known for its sweet, crisp flavor. Chantenay - A short, stubby carrot that is sweet and tender, making it ideal for juicing and canning. Imperator - A long, tapered carrot that is popular for its crunchy texture and sweet flavor.

Growth Habits: Carrots are a cool-season crop and do best when planted in the spring or fall. They require well-drained soil that is rich in organic matter and has a pH of 6.0 to 6.8. Carrots grow best in a sunny location but will tolerate some light shade.

Planting: Carrots can be seeded directly in the garden or started indoors and then transplanted later. When planting seeds directly in the garden, sow seeds 1/4 to 1/2 inch deep and 1 to 2 inches apart. Cover seeds with soil and water well. When starting seeds indoors, sow seeds in pots 4 to 6 weeks before the last spring frost. Transplant seedlings into the garden when they are 2 to 3 inches tall and the soil has warmed to at least 50°F.

Harvesting: Carrots are ready to harvest when they reach the desired size, typically about 70 to 80 days after planting. To harvest, simply pull carrots from the soil. For the best flavor, harvest carrots before they become too large.

Expected Yield: The expected yield of carrots varies depending on the variety, soil, and growing conditions. On average, you can expect to harvest 1 to 2 pounds of carrots per 10 feet of row.

Watering and Irrigation: Carrots need consistent moisture to grow well. Water regularly, keeping the soil evenly moist but not waterlogged. If the soil dries out too much, the carrots will become tough and woody.

Common Problems:

Root Maggots: Root maggots are small, white insects that feed on the roots of carrots. To prevent infestations, rotate crops and use insecticidal soap or companion planting with strongly scented plants.

Cracking: Cracking is a common problem when growing carrots. This occurs when the carrots grow too quickly or unevenly, causing the skin to split open. To prevent cracking, keep the soil evenly moist and plant in soil that is well-drained and has good water-holding capacity.

Celery

Different Types of Celery: There are several different types of celery, including Pascal, Golden Self-Blanching, and Tango. Pascal celery is the most common type and has a crisp, green stalk. Golden Self-Blanching celery is yellow in color and is less bitter than Pascal celery. Tango celery is a hybrid variety that is known for its high yields and crisp texture.

Growth Habits: Celery is a cool-season crop that thrives in moderate temperatures between 50°F and 70°F. It is sensitive to heat and can be damaged by temperatures above 80°F. Celery is also a heavy feeder and requires fertile soil with a pH range between 6.0 and 6.8. The soil should also be well-drained and consistently moist.

Planting: Celery should be started indoors about 4 to 6 weeks before the last frost date in your area. Transplant the seedlings into the garden when they are about 6 inches tall and the soil temperature is at least 60°F. Plant celery in rows that are spaced 18 to 24 inches apart. Space the plants within each row about 8 to 10 inches apart.

Harvesting: Celery is ready to harvest about 100 to 120 days after planting. Harvest the outer stalks first, leaving the center stalks to continue growing. When the center stalk reaches about 12 inches tall, you can harvest the entire plant.

Expected Yield: A single celery plant can produce between 6 and 8 stalks. A 100-foot row of celery can produce between 50 and 75 pounds of celery.

Watering and Irrigation: Celery requires consistent moisture to grow properly. Water the plants regularly, being careful not to overwater or allow the soil to dry out completely. A soaker hose or drip irrigation system is a good option for celery, as it helps prevent water from splashing on the leaves and causing disease.

Common Problems:

Fusarium Wilt: This disease is caused by a fungus that attacks the plant's roots, causing yellowing and wilting of the leaves. Fusarium Wilt can be prevented by using disease-resistant varieties, rotating crops, and avoiding planting in contaminated soil.

Root Maggots: To prevent root maggots, use floating row covers to protect the plants, and rotate crops to different areas of the garden each year.

Potatoes

Types of Potatoes: There are many different types of potatoes, including russet, red, yellow, and fingerling. Each type has its own unique flavor, texture, and cooking properties. Some types of potatoes are better suited for baking and others for frying.

Growth Habits: Potatoes grow best in a climate with moderate temperatures and adequate moisture. They are typically grown in USDA hardiness zones 3-9. The ideal soil for growing potatoes is well-drained, with a pH between 4.5 and 7. Potatoes prefer a loamy soil with good organic matter content.

Planting: Potatoes can be planted in the spring after the last frost has passed. To plant potatoes, select seed potatoes (small, mature potatoes) and cut them into pieces, each with at least one "eye" (bud). Let the cut pieces dry for a few days before planting them. Plant the seed potatoes about 4-6 inches deep in soil, spacing them about 12-15 inches apart. Cover the seed potatoes with soil and water well.

Harvesting: Potatoes are ready to harvest when the tops of the plants have died back. This usually happens about 80-100 days after planting. To harvest, carefully dig up the plants and collect the potatoes. Allow the harvested potatoes to cure in a warm, dry place for a few days before storing them.

Expected Yield: The expected yield of a potato crop can vary depending on the variety, the growing conditions, and the care given to the plants. On average, you can expect to harvest 5-10 pounds of potatoes per 10 feet of row.

Watering and Irrigation: Potatoes need to be kept evenly moist, but not waterlogged. Water your potato plants deeply once a week, or more frequently during hot, dry weather.

Common Problems

Early Blight: This fungal disease affects the leaves and stems of potato plants. Symptoms include brown spots on the leaves and wilting of the plant. To prevent early blight, rotate your potato crop every few years and avoid overhead watering.

Potato Scab: This disease affects the skin of the potato and makes it rough and scabby. To prevent potato scab, plant resistant varieties and maintain a pH of 6.0-7.0 in the soil.

ONION

Types of Onions

Yellow Onions: These are the most common type of onion and have a strong, pungent flavor. They are versatile in cooking and are used in a variety of dishes, such as soups and stews.

White Onions: White onions have a sweeter and milder flavor than yellow onions, making them a great option for salads and raw dishes.

Red Onions: Red onions have a mild and sweet flavor and are often used in salsa and salads. They also add a pop of color to any dish.

Sweet Onions: As their name suggests, sweet onions have a very sweet flavor, making them a great option for eating raw or in salads.

Growth Habits: Onions are cool-season biennials that are typically grown as annuals. They prefer a good amount of sunlight, about 6-8 hours per day to grow properly.

Climate and Soil: Onions grow best in a moderate climate with temperatures between 60-75°F. They prefer well-draining soil that is rich in organic matter. The soil pH should be between 6.0-6.8.

Planting: Onions are typically planted in the early spring and can be planted from sets (small bulb onions), seeds, or transplants. When planting from sets, plant them about 1 inch deep and 4 inches apart. When planting from seeds, sow them about 1/4 inch deep and thin the seedlings to 4 inches apart once they have sprouted. When planting from transplants, plant them about 4 inches apart and 1 inch deep.

Harvesting: Onions are typically ready to harvest when the tops have fallen over and have turned yellow. This typically takes between 95-110 days from planting. To harvest, gently pull the onions from the ground and let them dry in the sun for a few days before storing them.

Expected Yield: On average, you can expect to harvest about 10-15 pounds of onions per 10 feet of row.

Watering and Irrigation: Onions require consistent moisture and should be watered deeply once a week, or more often during hot, dry weather. Ensure that the soil does not dry out completely as this can cause the onions to become tough and woody.

Common Problems:

Onion Maggot: Onion maggots are small fly larvae that feed on the bulbs of onions. To prevent an infestation, cover the soil around the onions with a barrier, such as row covers, to prevent the flies from laying their eggs.

Botrytis Blight: Botrytis blight is a fungal disease that can cause the leaves of onions to turn brown and rot. To prevent this, avoid planting onions in areas where other members of the Allium family have been grown recently and practice good garden hygiene, such as removing and destroying any infected leaves.

How To Diagnose & Solve Common Gardening Issues

Plants are living organisms and, as such, are exposed to various diseases that affect garden plants, potted plants or those in your vegetable garden. It is important to know how to recognize the symptoms of different plant diseases so that you can intervene promptly and effectively. Color changes or leaf changes are the first alarm bells that alert us to a plant disease; it is good to learn to observe them to catch the first symptoms. There are several causes for which plants can become diseased, and the main ones are:

- Poor care or cultivation: water stagnation, wrong positioning or fertilization;
- Insects or pests: aphids, bugs, caterpillars;
- Fungi: powdery mildew, gray mold, plant rust;
- Climatic conditions: special weather conditions or adverse weather phenomena.

How to Avoid Plant Diseases

Taking care of our plants means controlling several factors that affect their health. Typical mistakes that lead the plant to get sick are incorrect watering or exposure, which in the long run, if not corrected, can even lead to the death of the plant. If we notice blanched leaves the plant is probably suffering from too much direct sun exposure. On the contrary if the plant has little sun exposure for its needs we will have yellowing of the leaves. Even if the plant is suffering from insufficient fertilization or unsuitable soil we will always tell by its leaves, which will look crumpled. Poor care can also lead to mold growth. Water stagnation and poorly airy environments can cause what is known as gray mold, which is observed by whitish spots on the leaves.

Plant Diseases By Unwanted Guests

The worst nightmare for those who grow garden or vegetable plants are infestations due to small insects or pests that cause various plant diseases. Aphids or plant lice are perhaps the best known. They particularly affect roses and can be seen with the naked eye. Aphids suck sap through the soft parts of plants and are easily seen precisely because these tiny insects cover the plant. If, on the other hand, we notice eaten or pitted leaves, our plants are probably infested with bugs or caterpillars.

Another pest that affects garden and ornamental plants indifferently is the White Fly. This is a very small pest that causes white or yellow spots on leaves and shows the first symptoms when the infestation is quite advanced.

FUNGAL PLANT DISEASES

In addition to the gray mold we have already discussed, there are other fungi that can attack plants under particular conditions.

Powdery mildew, also known as white mildew, strikes mainly in spring when temperatures are not yet too high, or in autumn, before the big cold weather arrives. In fact, it develops in hot, humid climates and when there is not good ventilation. It is recognizable by the grayish-white powdery-looking spots that occur on the leaves until they dry out.

Another plant disease due to fungi is the so-called plant rust, which is actually caused by different types of fungi that have the same peculiarity: they form a brownish-colored powdery patina on the leaves, similar precisely to rust.

MOST COMMON PEST & DISEASE

APHIDS
SAP-SUCKING INSECT

REMEDIES
- **Organic**: Ludwig's Insect Spray, Biogrow Bioneem, Biogrow Vegol
- **Non-organic**: Efekto Aphicide, Efekto Rosecare, Makhro Plantcare

Aphids come in a large variety of shapes and colours. Have many natural predators.

LILY BORER
CATEPILLAR

REMEDIES
- **Organic**: Margaret Roberts Caterpillar Insecticide
- **Non-organic**: Cypermethrin, Protek Knox Worm

Prevalent in plants of the Lily family, especially Amaryllis & Agapanthus

CHAFER BEETLE
LEAF EATING INSECT

REMEDIES
- **Organic**: Ludwig's Insecticide
- **Non-organic**: Karba Spray, Efekto Garden Gun, Starke Ayres Garden Insect Spray

Active at night in summer. Prevalent on roses, vegetables and birches.

WOOLLY APHID
SAP-SUCKING INSECT

REMEDIES
- **Organic**: Biogrow Pyrol, Makhro Sk Eco Oil, Efekto Oleum
- **Non-organic**: Efekto Insecticide Granules, Plant Protector

Occur on ornamentals as well as vegetables and fruit.

PSYLLA
SAP-SUCKING INSECT

REMEDIES
- **Organic**: Biogrow Neudosan
- **Non-organic**: Protek Koinor, Efekto Aphicide

Although unsightly, only a severe infestation will affect the health of the plant.

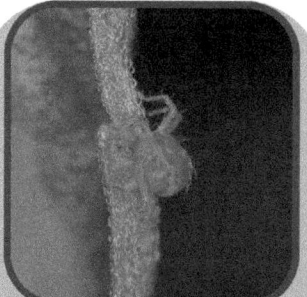

RED SPIDER MITE
SAP-SUCKING INSECT

REMEDIES
- **Organic**: Biogrow Pyrol, Makhro Organicide, Efekto Eco Fungimite
- **Non-organic**: Makhro Plantcare, Efekto Rosecare

Fine red lacy appearance on undersides of leave

SNAILS & SLUGS
MOLLUSCS

REMEDIES
- **Organic**: Biogrow Ferramol, Efekto Eco Snail & Slug Trap
- **Non-organic**: Efekto Snailban, Snailflo

To prevent, create a habitat for natural enemies and rectify soil pH

WHITEFLY
SAP SUCKING INSECT

REMEDIES
- **Organic**: Margaret Roberts Insecticide, Biogrow Pyrol
- **Non-organic**: Makhro Plantcare, Efekto Plant Protector

Looks like a white powder underneath leaves, but will fly off if leaves are shaken.

SCALE
SAP-SUCKING INSECT

REMEDIES
- **Organic**: Biogrow Pyrol, Makhro Sk Eco Oil, Efekto Oleum
- **Non-organic**: Efekto Insecticide Granules, Plant Protector

Occur on ornamentals as well as vegetables and fruit.

POWDERY MILDEW
FUNGAL DISEASE

REMEDIES
- **Organic**: Ludwig's Copper Count, Margaret Roberts Organic Fungicide, Biogrow Copper Soap
- **Non-organic**: Efekto Rosecare, Funginex, Verikop

Looks like spots of white powder mostly on upper surfaces of leaves.

BLACK SPOT
FUNGAL DISEASE

REMEDIES
- **Organic**: Ludwig's Copper Count, Margaret Roberts Organic Fungicide, Biogrow Copper Soap
- **Non-organic**: Efekto Rosecare, Funginex, Verikop

Dark spots of dead tissue on leaves.

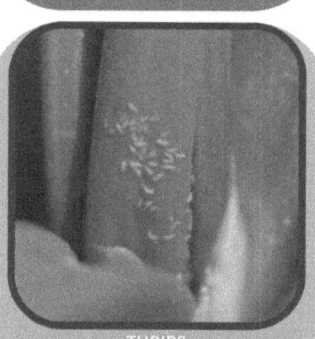

THRIPS
SAP SUCKING INSECT

REMEDIES
- **Organic**: Ludwig's Insect Spray, Efekto Eco Insect Control
- **Non-organic**: Cypermethrine, Malasol

Can appear as tiny, winged insects or pale worms.

Climatic Conditions Favoring Plant Diseases

As we have already seen, the good positioning of the plant is very important for its well-being. However, there are climatic conditions that can make even well-maintained and protected plants sick.

Probably few people are aware of plant heat stroke. In fact, in very hot and dry summers some types of plants, vines for example, can suffer from dehydration and excessive sunlight. Symptoms show up as yellowing and desiccation of a portion of the plant, and if no action is taken it can lead to the death of the fruit or the plant itself.

Then there are the sudden and violent weather events, such as frosts and damaging hailstorms, against which we can only take preventive action by protecting our vegetable garden and garden plants.

Plant Nutritional Deficiencies

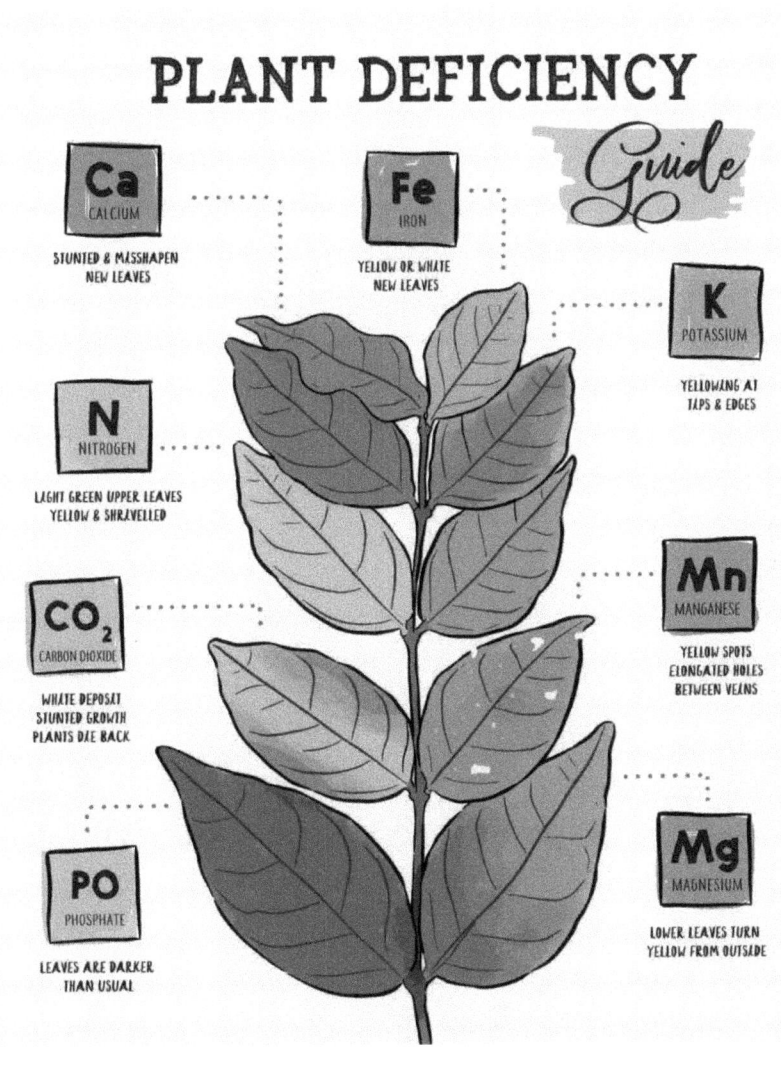

Lack of just one of the nutrients produces a whole series of deficiency symptoms that, if prolonged over time, lead to stunted growth and eventually plant death. Nutrient deficiencies affect all plants, both garden and vegetable gardens, indoors and outdoors. Diagnosis of a disease is a delicate matter, and one should not dwell on the superficiality of a single symptom. Generally, nutritional deficiency is evident on the plant with manifestations on the leaves (including the underside), flowers, stems, fruits, and general bearing. However, symptoms are not always immediately identifiable. For this reason, complete microelement fertilizers are always recommended, while if the deficiency is to be treated, specific products should be used. Sometimes a deficiency is a consequence of a pest infestation, and work on a possible pest infestation needs to be worked on before efforts are made to sustain the plant and bring it back to a fully healthy state.

Low CO2 Levels - Plants grown with low CO2 levels have problems with photosynthesis, old leaves fall early, and overall growth stunts.

- Mature leaves fall off early
- The plant loses its green color, turning from yellow to white.

CO2 Excess - A higher-than-normal C02 concentration brings enormous benefits to the plant: it speeds up its metabolism and consequently results in a higher yield. The plant produces in greater quantities and faster. In addition, a higher C02 level makes the plant stronger and less sensitive to environmental stresses and pollution.

However, if your plant crop receives too much C02, the benefits mentioned above are lost. Excessively high levels of carbon dioxide result in slowdowns for plant growth. Therefore, it is essential to constantly monitor C02 levels (also because in high amounts it becomes toxic even to people).

Nitrogen (N) deficiency - Nitrogen-deficient plants have slowed growth; older leaves cannot produce chlorophyll and turn yellow between the veins, while the veins remain green. Yellowing continues over the entire leaf until it falls off. Sometimes the leaves and branches may turn reddish, which leads to confusing nitrogen deficiency with phosphorus deficiency. Nitrogen is a very mobile element and is consumed quickly, so it should be added regularly through slow-release fertilizers.

- Old leaves and yellowing between the veins that can gradually extend
- Branches and leaf veins may turn red-purple
- Young leaves develop intervening chlorosis
- Leaf drop

Nitrogen Excess - Leaves turn dark green and tend to have a glossy appearance, enclose deforming while branches have longer internodes. This leads the plant to be more susceptible to insect attacks such as aphids and fungal infections. The plant absorbs less water. If it is severe, the leaves turn a bronze-copper color. The roots develop more slowly and rot. Flowers are smaller and ripe fruits split.

Phosphorus (P) deficiency - Plants with Phosphorus deficiency have slowed growth. Leaves are small, bluish green and often spotted. Stems, leaves and veins turn reddish from the edges and back. The reddening, however, is not always pronounced. Old leaves become dark and curled, and the edges curl. If the deficiency is severe, the leaves develop large dark purple spots that later turn bronze, dry shrivel, and fall off. The deficiency is aggravated in clay or acidic soils, and the most common deficiency is when the substrate has a pH level above 7. With a pH level below 5.8 and with excess zinc and iron, phosphates are not assimilated by the plant.

- Chlorosis along leaf veins (starting with young leaves).
- Leaves turn bronze-purple, shrivel and die
- Dark bluish-green leaves often with dark spots
- Stunted growth

Phosphorus Excess - Plants are very susceptible to disease and mold, and there is an unusual growth of apicals. Plants can take weeks to manifest excess. It also manifests as zinc deficiency.

Potassium (K) Deficiency - Potassium (mobile element) deficiency occasionally occurs in both indoor and outdoor growing media in soil, but rarely in hydroponic crops. The potassium-deficient plant develops yellow edges and chlorotic spots on the leaves (similar to calcium deficiency but only on the leaf edge), and the lower leaves die or turn light brown. The plant becomes susceptible to diseases. Potassium is usually present in the soil however it is often blocked by the high salinity of the substrate itself. It increases the internal temperature of the leaves causing the degradation of cellular proteins. Excessive evaporation from leaf margins causes red scorch associated with same-colored stems.

- Old leaves lose luster and develop russet spots
- Leaf margins become dry, brown and raised
- Delayed and much reduced flowering
- Branches and stems become very thin

Potassium excess - This is difficult to diagnose; usually the leaves turn bright yellow to white. When uptake of magnesium, manganese-and sometimes Zinc and Iron-is slow or nil, there is almost always an excess of potassium. Excess is treated by light fertilization with the other trace elements.

Magnesium (Mg) deficiency - Magnesium (mobile element) deficiency in plants is usually made evident in the middle or lower leaves of the plant, then spreads to the younger leaves. Leaves turn yellow or white with veins that remain dark green-these are the most obvious indicators of a magnesium deficiency. Lower and middle leaves develop yellow patches between the dark green veins. Leaf margins bend before the leaf falls off. The plant may turn yellow within a few weeks, and if severe it turns completely white. Magnesium deficiency is uncommon in outdoor crops.

- Patchy chlorosis (starting on old leaves)
- Early loss of older leaves
- Upward folding of leaf margins
- Yellowish or purplish blotches on the leaf blade

Magnesium excess - Excess Magnesium is rarely seen; moreover, it is difficult to diagnose with the naked eye.

Calcium (Ca) deficiency - Calcium deficiency in a plant can affect the soil by causing it to become too acidic. It is very abundant in nature and is found in the form of limestone ($CaCO_3$), so any deficiencies can be found in acidic soils. Internerval deformation and chlorosis can be observed on leaves, as well as desiccation of vegetative apices and leaf margins.

- Chlorosis of young leaves, followed by necrosis and drooping
- Dull leaf color, yellowing
- Deformed leaves
- Bending and wilting of leaf edges

Calcium Excess - Soil basification, resulting in deficiencies of K, N, Mg, and ferric chlorosis with leaf necrosis. Excess manifests, especially in acidophilic species, with yellowing of leaves.

Iron (Fe) Deficiency - Iron deficiency in plants begins with new leaves and is typically signaled by internerval chlorosis, which can develop into widespread discoloration of apical leaves. It is common when the pH level is above 6.5. Symptoms may appear during periods of strong growth or stress. The veins remain green while the inner areas turn yellow. Chlorosis gradually becomes more acute and, in severe cases, leaves fall off. Some plants, acidophiles may have iron deficiency problems if planted in neutral or basic soils.

- Very pronounced chlorosis of young leaves starting at the veins.
- Yellowing also spreads to older leaves
- Necrosis of leaves develops

Iron excess: Excess is rare; however, it can interfere with the uptake of phosphorus and other elements. Excesses cause bronze leaves and brown spots, even to the point of plant death.

Manganese (Mn) deficiency - Manganese (nonmoving element) deficiency is rare and is almost always associated with iron and zinc deficiency; it manifests in intervening areas that turn yellow while the veins remain green. Symptoms then spread to older leaves. Necrotic areas may develop on the heavily affected leaves, which then fall off. The plant appears wilted.

- Intervening chlorosis on new leaves.
- Necrotic zones develop on the very affected leaves.
- Growth is slowed and apices are shriveled

Manganese excess - New leaves and apices develop a rusty-orange color that then spreads to old leaves. Slowed growth and iron and zinc deficiency.

Conclusion

In conclusion, vegetable gardening is not only a fulfilling hobby but also a valuable life skill that has stood the test of time. By mastering the basics of soil preparation, plant selection, and proper watering and fertilization techniques, you can reap the benefits of growing your own fresh, nutrient-rich produce right in your own backyard.

Gardening allows you to connect with nature and experience the satisfaction of watching your seeds blossom into healthy, thriving plants. Furthermore, growing your own vegetables provides a sense of independence, as you can control the quality and safety of the food you eat. Whether you are a seasoned gardener or just starting out, there is always something new to learn and discover in the world of vegetable gardening.

So, don't be afraid to dive in and start your journey today! You will be amazed at the personal and environmental rewards that come with growing your own food.

BOOK 2:

Organic Vegetable Gardening

Introduction

Organic gardening is a method of growing plants and crops without the use of synthetic chemicals and fertilizers. Instead, organic gardeners use natural substances and techniques to create a healthy and sustainable growing environment. The goal of organic gardening is to produce healthy and nutritious food while also preserving and enhancing the environment.

This growing model relies on building healthy soil, controlling pests and diseases with natural methods, and using compost and other organic matter to provide nutrients to plants. Organic gardeners also use crop rotation, companion planting, and other techniques to promote soil health and reduce pest and disease problems.

There are many benefits to organic gardening. Organic food is healthier, as it is grown without harmful chemicals and has been shown to contain higher levels of nutrients than conventionally grown food. Organic gardening also helps to conserve natural resources, such as water and soil, and reduces pollution from chemical fertilizers and pesticides. Additionally, organic gardening provides a way to connect with nature and create a healthier and more sustainable environment for future generations.

Soil Health

Organic farming takes its example from what happens in nature: if plants are able to self-regulate to have ever-fertile soil, it is necessary to imitate them. In a forest, leaves fall to the ground and are eaten by insects, decomposed by aerobic bacteria and turned into humus. So in organic horticulture we need to know how to bring in organic matter and work the soil without breaking its balance. Therefore, to understand how to best do an organic vegetable garden, we need to start with taking care of the soil, and analyzing the soil so that we know how to work it to make it best cultivable. Fertility and proper soil structure are crucial elements for the proper cultivation of the vegetable garden. In the organic method this is doubly important: by renouncing the use of toxic chemicals, one bets on the action of the microorganisms residing in the soil. A draining and healthy soil make it possible to prevent most plant diseases.

HOW TO ANALYZE YOUR SOIL

Before starting to garden, it is very important to go and analyze the soil you are going to grow. Those who are organic horticulturists by passion certainly cannot afford expensive laboratory tests that go into investigating the composition of the soil you have.

However, one can still rely on some rather simple empirical tests. In this way it is possible to get an idea regarding the main characteristics of the soil and set up farming accordingly.

Conversely, those who grow vegetables or fruit trees for income may have compensated for having a professional soil test done; this is an investment that allows you to study expedients aimed at obtaining better yields.

Simple observation

Initial assessments of a soil are made without the need for any experiments or instrumentation, but simply by observing and noting climatic conditions, response to rainfall, and the presence of water.

Climatic conditions. Soil analysis must go hand in hand with an assessment of the climatic conditions to which crop plants will be subjected. It is necessary to assess the exposure to the sun, to understand how many hours of light the crops will have, and to know what the minimum and maximum temperatures are during the various seasons, in order to be able to adjust for the planting period. The garden design will necessarily have to take all this information into account.

Response to rainfall. Another important observation to make is how the soil responds to rainfall: just go to the plot during a day of heavy rainfall and try to observe how quickly the soil absorbs rainwater, and if there are any spots where stagnation (puddles or slush) forms. Continue to observe the vegetable garden in the following days to observe its ability to retain moisture and drain excess water quickly.

Presence of water. Another important check before planting is whether we have water available.

Identifying Wild Grasses

Even by looking at what grasses grow on a soil we can get an idea of what kind of soil we are looking at. In fact, every species however adaptable it may be develops in an environment favorable to it. The wild grasses we find in the fields give us so much insight into the type of soil in which they grow. In fact, over time in each environment they tend to select the species that are best adapted to the soil parameters present such as texture, tendency or otherwise to waterlogging, ph, lime content, mineral element and organic matter content. If we learn to recognize some typical plants in uncultivated meadows, we can gain very important information about the soil in which we find them.

The wild species that grow in a fallow soil or on a perennial meadow are not the same as those that prevail on cultivated land.

The reasons are mainly related to human intervention in terms of tillage: an untilled soil tends to maintain its stratigraphy, its microbiological balances, and in some cases becomes very compacted, especially if it has a clay texture. Many species typical of compacted soils and in some cases moisture-loving species develop in such situations.

Steadily tilled soil, on the other hand, is a suitable environment for different species that like soils made crumbly and fertilized.

We will therefore notice that once a vegetable garden is started, the wild species will tend to change over time compared to what the same plot was in its natural state. But noting the prevalence of certain species gives us important clues that are useful to know before we start growing them.

The Measurement of Soil pH

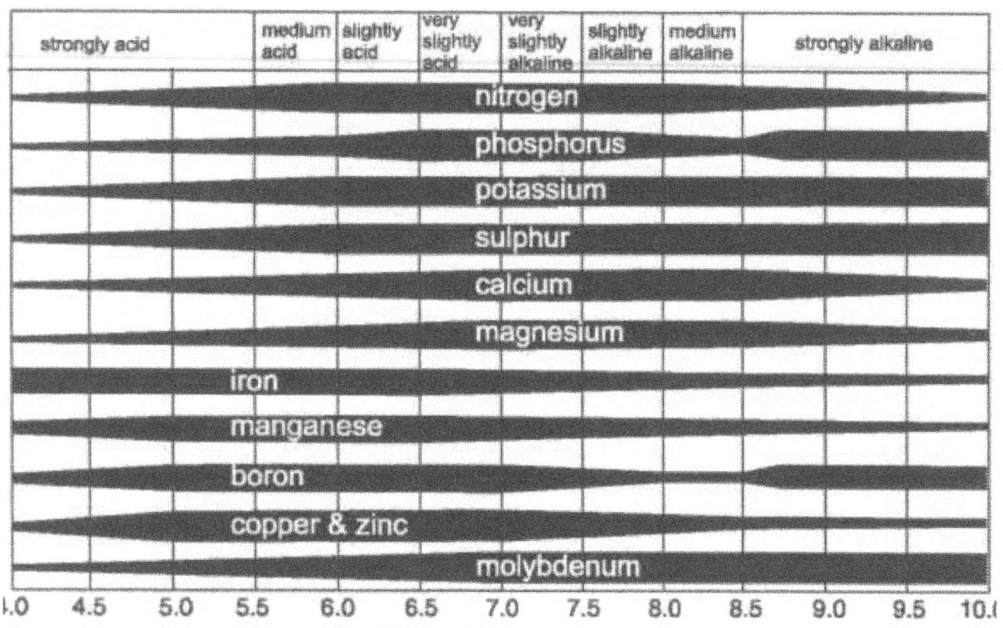

A very important fact about soil that we cannot determine at a glance is the ph value. This is a physical relationship that is decisive in favoring or not favoring the uptake of certain substances by plants, which is also related to the presence of calcium in the soil. Ph analysis can simply be done on one's own with the use of a litmus paper. If the soil is found to be too acidic or too basic, action can be taken to make a correction and make the soil more suitable for the plants we want to grow.

The pH score is not an abstract number-it is closely related to the presence of calcium, which is the most important of the trace elements that vegetables need to grow strong and healthy in our garden.

Every plant has a "preferred" pH value, which corresponds to the ideal condition for healthy living and development. Most vegetables ask for a neutral substrate, between 6 and 7, while small fruits are usually acidophilic plants, which prefer lower pH values, around 4.5 / 5.

In cash crop farming, soil analysis is done in the laboratory; in the family garden, one cannot often afford the expense involved in chemical analysis. However, we can learn how to study the characteristics of our soil in a homemade way, even to the point of doing a kind of soil analysis ourselves

Measuring the pH of the aqueous extract of soil is fortunately very easy to do "do-it-yourself," using litmus paper found in any pharmacy; alternatively, there are meters. Let's find out how to measure pH and especially what it means to have acidic or basic soil and what corrections can be made in organic farming.

What is PH?

The pH of the soil is a numerical measure of acidity, that is, the concentration of hydrogen ions (H+) in the so-called "liquid phase" of the soil, that is, the circulating solution.

The acidity of the soil is determined by the ratio of hydrogen ions to hydroxyl ions; chemical compounds dissolved in the water in the soil contribute to the variation of this value.

I'll stop with the big words, since in chemistry even I am not very well versed. What garden growers need to know is that pH has an important influence on a whole series of reactions that occur in nature and is decisive for the life of soil microorganisms. Consequently, it also has effects on the activity of the plant's root system and particularly on their ability to assimilate nutrients. The theoretical measure of pH ranges between zero and 14, where the lower the value, the more acidic the soil. Around 7 we have neutral soil while above that we have basic or alkaline soils.

- **Acidic soil:** ph below 7 (the lower the ph the more acidic the soil).
- **Neutral soil**: ph = 7.
- **Basic or alkaline soil:** ph greater than 7 (the higher the ph, the more basic the soil).

How to measure pH with a litmus paper

To measure soil pH on your own are basically 3:

- Take an average sample of the soil.
- Place the soil in distilled water.
- Use litmus paper.

These are very simple things, but they need to be done carefully so as not to invalidate the measurement. In particular, the taking of the sample is good to explain.

1. **How to take a representative soil sample** - First, wanting to measure ph correctly, one must obtain a soil sample that correctly represents the vegetable garden. Soil is not homogeneous, so if we want to get an average sample we have to take soil in several places (subsamples) and then mix. So we take 5 or 6 sub-samples at different points in the vegetable garden. You should not take soil that is too deep, but also not too shallow. Each sub-sample should be taken about 10 centimeters deep. If you have just fertilized, it makes little sense to measure the pH, because the reactions caused by the added organic matter will alter the values.

2. **Using litmus paper** - After taking the various samples let's mix them to get the average sample. A tablespoon of soil from this sample should be placed in a glass of distilled water, which will then be

shaken by stirring. For a more precise measurement, the ratio of 10 grams of soil for every 25 ml of water should be kept. It is important that the water be distilled because otherwise the composition of the water will alter the measurement.

3. **Determine soil pH:** Litmus paper is dipped into the solution of water and soil; the soaking time is specified on the package. Depending on the color that is detected on the litmus paper, the pH measurement is obtained.

Soil Ph levels for plant chart

Very acid (pH 5.0 to 5.8)	Moderately acid pH of 5.5 to 6.8)	Slightly acid (pH 6.0 to 6.8)	Very alkaline (pH 7.0 to 8.0)
azalea blueberry celeriac chickory crabapple cranberry eggplant endive heathers huckleberry hydrangea Irish potato lily lupine oak raspberry rhododendron rhubarb shallot sorrel spinach beet spruce wild strawberry sweet potato watermelon white birch	bean begonia Brussels sprouts calla camellia collard greens corn fuchsia garlic lima bean parsley pea peppers pumpkin radish rutabaga soybean squash sunflower turnip viola	asparagus beet bok choy broccoli cabbage carrot cauliflower celery cucumber gooseberry grape kale kohlrabi lettuce mustard muskmelon oats okra onion pansy beach peanut pear peony rhubarb rice spinach Swiss chard tomato zucchini	acacia date palms dusty miller eucalyptus geranium oleander olive periwinkle pinks pomegranate salt cedar tamarisk thyme

ORGANIC TECHNIQUES TO IMPROVE SOIL QUALITY

Compost

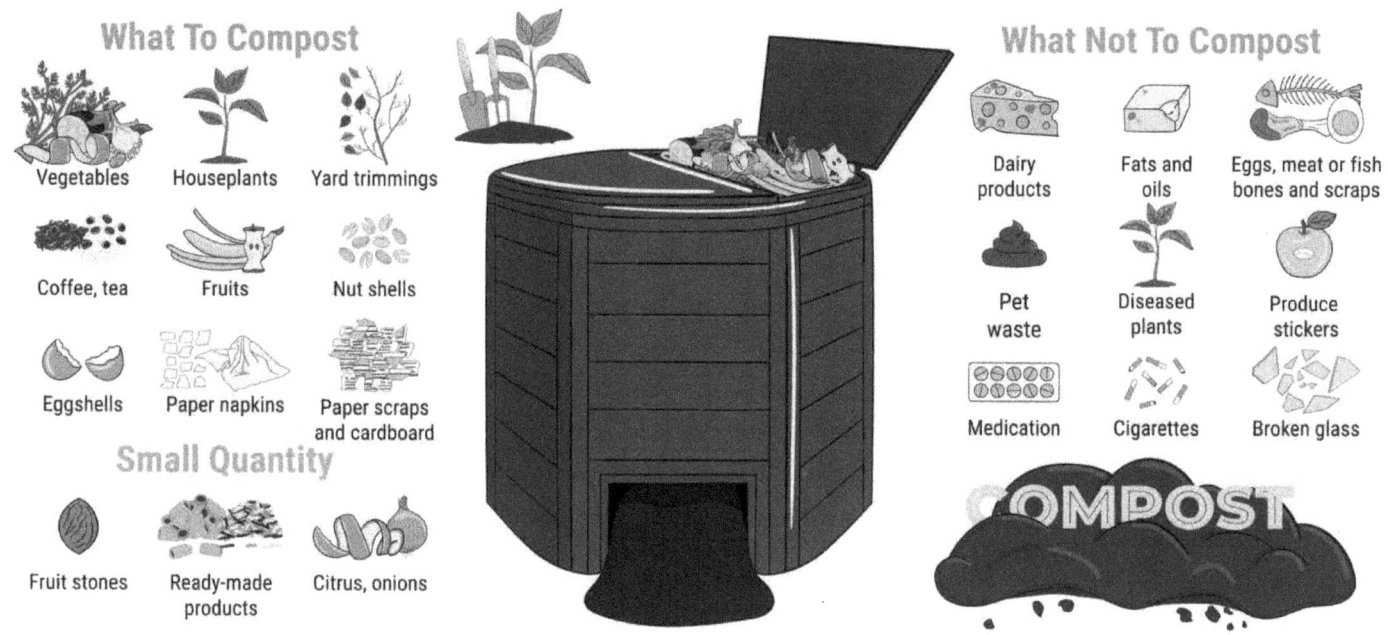

Compost is created by decomposing organic matter, such as leaves, grass clippings, and kitchen scraps, into a nutrient-rich soil amendment. In this chapter, we will explore the benefits of composting, how to make compost, and how to use it in your garden.

Benefits of Composting:

- Adds Nutrients to Soil: Compost contains a range of essential nutrients that plants need to grow, such as nitrogen, phosphorus, and potassium.

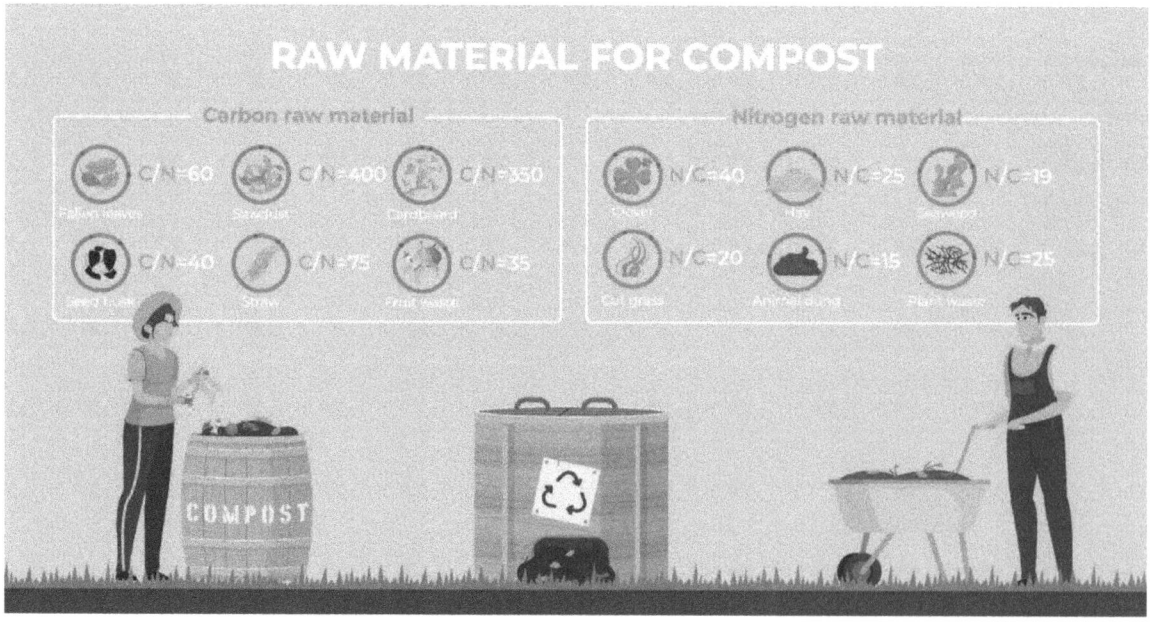

68

- Improves Soil Structure: Compost helps to improve soil structure by increasing the amount of organic matter in the soil. This in turn helps soil to retain moisture and nutrients, and can also improve soil drainage.

- Reduces Waste: Composting is an environmentally-friendly way to reduce waste and conserve natural resources. Instead of sending yard waste and food scraps to the landfill, they can be turned into a valuable resource for your garden

- Controls Pests and Diseases: Compost contains beneficial microorganisms that can help to control pests and diseases in your garden.

Making Compost:

1. **Choose a Compost Bin:** You can purchase a compost bin, or you can make your own by using wire fencing or pallets to create a compost pile.

2. **Add Ingredients:** To make compost, you will need a mix of "green" ingredients (such as fresh grass clippings and kitchen scraps) and "brown" ingredients (such as leaves and straw). These ingredients should be chopped or shredded to help them decompose faster.

3. **Keep it Moist:** Compost should be moist, but not too wet. If it is too dry, it will decompose slowly, and if it is too wet, it will start to smell.

4. **Turn the Pile:** To help the compost decompose more quickly, turn the pile every few weeks. This will help to aerate the pile and distribute moisture evenly.

Using Compost in Your Garden:

- Prepare Soil: Before planting, amend your soil with compost by mixing it in with the top few inches of soil.

- Top Dress Plants: You can also top dress established plants by spreading a layer of compost around the base of the plant.

- Use as Mulch: Compost can also be used as mulch around plants to help retain moisture and control weeds.

Cover Crops

Cover crops are plants that are grown specifically to improve the quality of soil. They are not grown for consumption, but rather for the purpose of replenishing soil nutrients, suppressing weeds, improving soil structure, and reducing erosion. The use of cover crops is an important component of sustainable agriculture and organic gardening, and it is a technique that has been used for centuries to improve soil health.

How it Works

Cover crops work by putting a lot of energy into the soil through their root growth. As they grow, they take up excess nutrients from the soil, reducing soil fertility and weed growth. When the cover crops are turned under the soil, they release those nutrients back into the soil, which then makes them available for the next crop. The roots of the cover crops also help to improve soil structure by creating channels for water and air to penetrate.

Types of Cover Crops

There are many different types of cover crops, each with its own unique characteristics. Some of the most commonly used cover crops include clovers, cereals, legumes, brassicas, and grasses. Clovers are excellent nitrogen fixers and are often used in rotation with nitrogen-hungry crops like corn. Cereals, such as oats and barley, are great for building organic matter and suppressing weeds. Legumes, such as alfalfa and beans, are excellent sources of nitrogen and are often used in rotation with nitrogen-hungry crops like corn. Brassicas, such as mustard and radish, are great for suppressing weeds and breaking up soil compaction. Grasses, such as rye and wheat, are great for suppressing weeds and improving soil structure.

When & How to Plant Cover Crops

The timing of planting cover crops is important, as it will impact their ability to provide benefits to the soil. In general, cover crops should be planted after the main crop has been harvested, or in the off-season between growing seasons. This allows the cover crops to grow and mature during the dormant period, so they can be turned under before the next crop is planted.

Cover crops are typically planted using a seed drill, which allows for accurate placement of the seeds and helps ensure good seed-to-soil contact. The seed rate will depend on the type of cover crop being used and the desired outcome. In general, a higher seed rate will result in a denser stand of cover crops, which can provide greater benefits to the soil.

Turning Under Cover Crops

Turning under cover crops is an important part of the process, as it releases the nutrients and organic matter back into the soil. This is typically done with a plow or cultivator, which tills the soil and incorporates the cover crops into the soil. The timing of this step is important, as it will impact the availability of nutrients for the next crop. In general, cover crops should be turned under when they are in the vegetative stage, which is when they are actively growing and putting energy into the soil.

Crop Rotation

Crop rotation is a technique used to improve soil quality by rotating different crops in a specific pattern from year to year. The main objective of crop rotation is to maintain soil fertility, prevent the buildup of pests and diseases, and improve soil structure.

Crop rotation works by alternating crops from different plant families in a specific pattern. Each plant family has unique requirements for nutrients and water, and rotating crops from different families helps to prevent soil depletion and maintain soil health. Crop rotation also helps to reduce the buildup of soil-borne diseases and pests, which can have a major impact on crop yield and quality. When planning a crop rotation, it is important to consider the following factors:

- **Crop family:** Different crops belong to different plant families and have different requirements for nutrients and water. It is important to group crops into families and rotates crops from different families to prevent soil depletion and maintain soil health.

- **Crop length:** The length of time that a crop will be grown in a specific location should be considered when planning a crop rotation. Some crops, such as potatoes, are typically grown for several months, while others, such as lettuce, are typically grown for just a few weeks.

- **Crop type:** Different crop types, such as root crops, leafy greens, and fruiting vegetables, have different requirements for nutrients and water. It is important to consider these requirements when planning a crop rotation.

- **Soil type:** Different soil types have different properties and can affect crop growth and yield. It is important to consider the soil type when planning a crop rotation.

A typical crop rotation for a vegetable garden might include the following sequence:

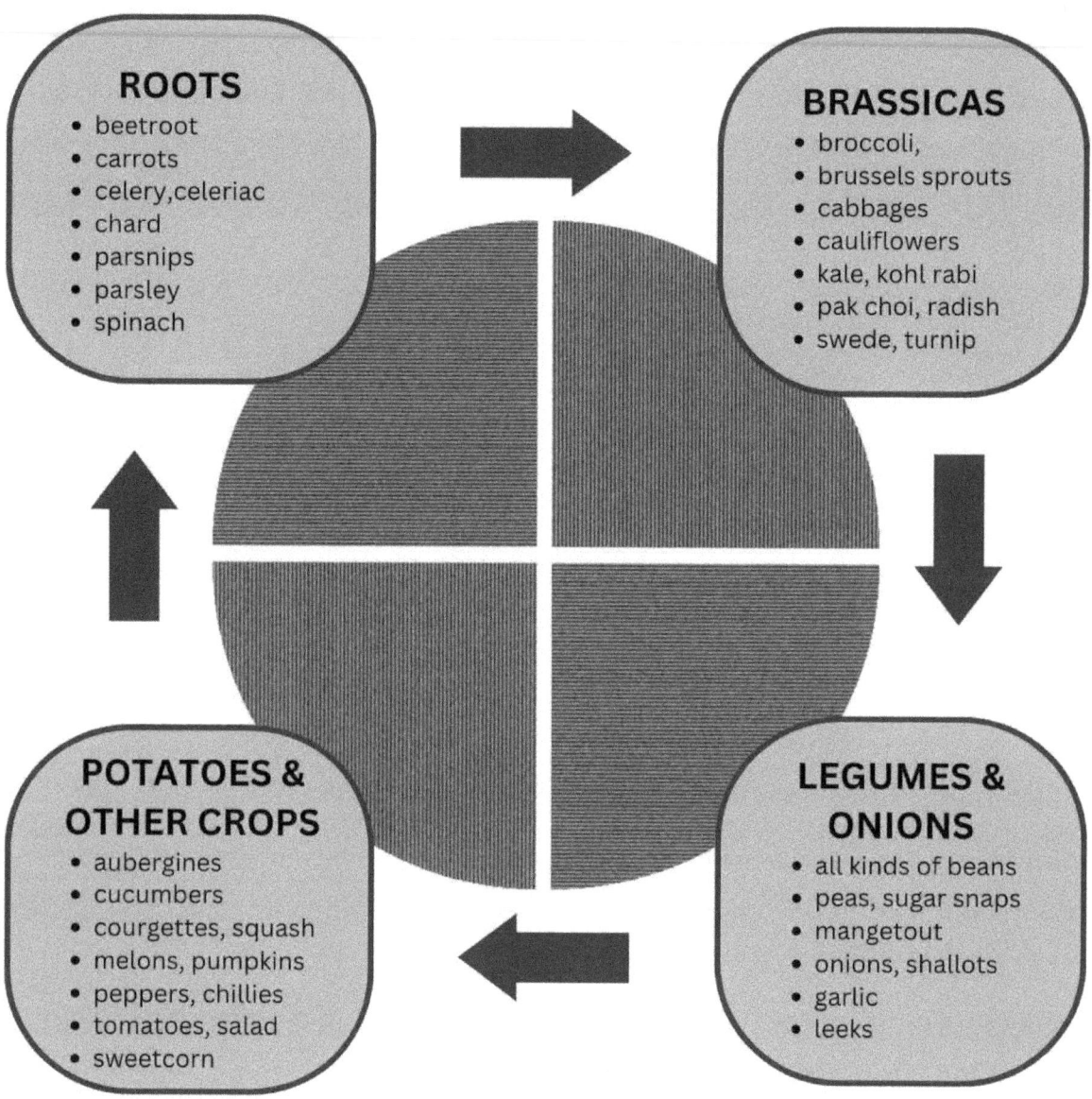

It is important to note that this is just an example and that the specific crop rotation will vary based on factors such as climate, soil type, and the specific crops being grown. In addition to improving soil quality, crop rotation can also have other benefits, such as increased yields, improved pest and disease management, and reduced soil erosion. By rotating crops in a thoughtful and systematic manner, gardeners can help to maintain soil fertility and improve the overall health of their soil.

In conclusion, soil health is the foundation of successful organic cultivation. By understanding and implementing the principles of soil health, you can create a thriving and sustainable environment that supports the growth of healthy and nutritious crops. From building soil structure and fertility through the use of organic matter, to promoting soil biodiversity through crop rotation and cover cropping, there are many practices that you can use to enhance the health of your soil. By doing so, you will not only improve the yields of your crops but also contribute to the preservation of the environment for future generations. So, embrace the principles of soil health and take your organic cultivation to the next level. With a little time, effort, and patience, you will be rewarded with a bountiful harvest of healthy and delicious crops grown in harmony with nature.

Natural Pest & Disease Control

In this chapter, we will delve into the topic of natural pest and disease control, a crucial aspect of sustainable agriculture. As the demand for organic and chemical-free produce continues to grow, it is increasingly important to understand the various methods that can be used to maintain healthy crops without relying on harmful pesticides and fertilizers.

From utilizing beneficial insects to implementing cultural practices, this chapter will explore the various ways to keep crops safe from pests and diseases without sacrificing the health of the environment. With a focus on holistic and integrated approaches, this chapter will provide insights into the importance of using natural pest and disease control methods in modern agriculture.

COMPANION PLANTING

Companion planting is a method of growing different types of plants together in the same garden or field, with the goal of improving the overall health and productivity of the plants. By selecting plants that have complementary relationships, companion planting can improve soil health, deter pests, and provide support for weaker plants.

Benefits of Companion Planting

- **Improved Soil Health:** Companion planting can help improve soil health by introducing different types of plants with different root systems, which can help to break up hardpan, prevent soil erosion, and improve soil structure.

- **Pest Deterrent:** Certain plants have natural pest-deterrent properties that can help protect other plants in the same area. For example, marigolds are often planted near tomatoes to deter aphids and other pests.

- **Nutrient Cycling:** Different types of plants have different nutrient requirements, and companion planting can help to balance the nutrients in the soil by providing plants with the right type of food.

- **Improved Yields:** Companion planting can also improve yields by providing plants with better growing conditions, such as increased sunlight, improved soil health, and improved pest control.

Best plant Alliances in Companion Planting

These are just a few examples of the best plant alliances in companion planting, and there are many other combinations that can be effective depending on your specific growing conditions and goals.

- **Beans and Corn:** Beans and corn make a great companion planting combination as the beans fix nitrogen in the soil, which is essential for the growth of corn.

- **Lettuce and Radishes:** Lettuce and radishes are often planted together because the fast-growing radishes help to improve soil structure for the slower-growing lettuce.

- **Marigolds and Vegetables:** Marigolds are often planted near vegetables to deter pests, such as aphids, and to improve the health of the soil.

- **Squash and Beans:** Squash and beans make a great companion planting combination as the beans help to provide support for the heavy squashes, while the large leaves of the squash help to shade the soil and conserve moisture.

- **Peas and Carrots:** Peas and carrots make a great companion planting combination as the peas help to improve soil health and provide a natural trellis for the carrots.

- **Garlic and Roses:** Garlic is often planted near roses to deter pests and improve the health of the soil.

- **Nasturtiums and Cabbages:** Nasturtiums are often planted near cabbages to deter pests, such as aphids, and to improve the health of the soil.

Companion planting is a simple and effective way to improve the health and productivity of your garden or farm. By selecting plants that have complementary relationships, you can enjoy a more diverse and sustainable ecosystem, with improved yields and healthier soil. Whether you are a beginner or an experienced gardener, companion planting is an important tool that can help you to achieve your goals and get the most out of your garden.

BENEFICIAL PLANT INSECTS & THEIR ROLE

Beneficial insects play a crucial role in maintaining the balance of ecosystems, including agricultural systems. These insects help control populations of harmful pests, pollinate crops, and decompose organic matter, among other important functions. Understanding the role of beneficial insects and the mechanisms that make them effective is key to promoting sustainable agriculture and preserving the health of the environment.

Types of Beneficial Insects

There are several types of beneficial insects, each with its own unique role in the ecosystem. Some of the most common beneficial insects include:

- **Pollinators:** Pollinators, such as bees and butterflies, play an important role in pollinating plants, which is essential for producing fruits, seeds, and nuts.

- **Parasitoids:** Parasitoids are insects that lay their eggs on or inside of pests. The parasitoid larvae then feed on the pests, killing them.

- **Predators:** Predatory insects, such as ladybugs and lacewings, feed on other insects, including harmful pests, thus reducing the population of the pests.

- **Decomposers:** Decomposers, such as dung beetles, feed on organic matter, breaking it down into simpler compounds, which enrich the soil and help maintain the soil's structure.

Functions of Beneficial Insects

Pest Control: Beneficial insects play a critical role in controlling populations of harmful pests. By preying on pests, beneficial insects can help keep populations in check, reducing the need for chemical pesticides.

- **Pollination:** Pollinators, such as bees and butterflies, play an important role in pollinating plants, which is essential for producing fruits, seeds, and nuts. This makes pollinators crucial to food production and the overall health of the ecosystem.

- **Soil Fertility:** Decomposers play an important role in breaking down organic matter and enriching the soil, helping to maintain soil structure and fertility.

- **Biodiversity:** Beneficial insects help maintain biodiversity in agricultural systems by promoting healthy populations of both pests and their natural predators.

Factors Affecting Beneficial Insect Populations

There are several factors that can affect the populations of beneficial insects, including:

- **Chemical Pesticides:** The use of chemical pesticides can have a negative impact on beneficial insect populations by killing both pests and their natural predators.

- **Habitat Destruction:** Destruction of habitats, such as the destruction of wetlands or the removal of hedgerows, can reduce the availability of food and shelter for beneficial insects.

- **Climate Change:** Climate change can have a significant impact on beneficial insect populations, changing their migration patterns, altering the timing of their life cycles, and reducing the availability of food.

How to Promote Beneficial Insect Populations

There are several ways to promote beneficial insect populations and maintain their populations in agricultural systems, including:

- **Reduce the Use of Chemical Pesticides:** By reducing the use of chemical pesticides, farmers can promote the survival and population growth of beneficial insects.

- **Create Habitats:** Creating habitats, such as flower gardens, can provide food and shelter for beneficial insects, helping to promote their populations.

- **Use Integrated Pest Management:** Integrated Pest Management (IPM) is a holistic approach to pest control that emphasizes the use of natural predators and cultural practices, rather than chemical pesticides, to control pest populations.

- **Practice Crop Rotation:** By rotating crops, farmers can help reduce the populations of harmful pests and promote the populations of beneficial insects.

Beneficial insect chart

INSECTS	PREYS ON	ATTRACTED BY
DAMSEL BUGS	• CATERPILLARS • MITES • APHIDS • CABBAGE WORMS	• CARAWAY • PETER PAN GOLDENROD • SPEARMINT • FENNEL
APHID MIDGES	• APHIDS	• DILL • PLANTS WITH PLENTY OF NECTAR AND POLLEN
MINUTE PIRATE BUGS	• SPIDER MITES • APHIDS • THRIPS • CATERPILLARS	• CARAWAY • FENNEL • ALFALFA • SPEARMINT
BRACONID WASPS	• CATERPILLARS • APHIDS	• FERN-LEAF YARROW • LEMON BALM • PARSLEY • COMMON YARROW
GROUND BEETLES	• SLUGS • CATERPILLARS • COLORADO POTATO BEETLES • CUTWORMS	• EVENING PRIMROSE • AMARANTHUS • CLOVER
LADYBUGS	• APHIDS • WHITEFLIES • COLORADO POTATO BEETLES	• DILL • DANDELION • FERN-LEAFYELLOW • BASKET OF GOLD
GREEN LACEWINGS	• APHIDS • WHITEFLIES • LEAFHOPPERS • MEALYBUGS	• DILL • ANGELICA • GOLDEN MARGUERITE • CORIANDER

In conclusion, beneficial insects play a critical role in maintaining the balance of agricultural ecosystems. By controlling populations of harmful pests, pollinating crops, and decomposing organic matter, beneficial insects help promote sustainable agriculture and protect the environment. To maintain healthy populations of beneficial insects, it is important to reduce the use of chemical pesticides, create habitats, practice integrated pest management, and implement crop rotation. By understanding the role and functions of beneficial insects, farmers and gardeners can take steps to promote their populations and ensure the health of their crops and the environment.

ORGANIC SPRAYS & DUSTS

Organic sprays and dusts are a type of pest control method that is becoming increasingly popular due to concerns about the health and environmental impacts of chemical pesticides. Organic sprays and dusts are made from natural ingredients, such as plant extracts and minerals, and are designed to control pests and diseases without harming the environment or human health. In this chapter, we will explore the different types of organic sprays and dusts, their functions, and the factors that influence their effectiveness.

Types of Organic Sprays and Dusts

Botanical Sprays: Botanical sprays are made from extracts of plants that have natural insecticidal or fungicidal properties. Some common botanical sprays include pyrethrin, neem oil, and garlic.

- **Mineral Dusts:** Mineral dusts are made from minerals, such as diatomaceous earth and kaolin, that have insecticidal properties. When applied to plants, the sharp edges of the minerals cut through the exoskeleton of pests, causing them to dehydrate and die.
- **Soap Sprays:** Soap sprays are made from soap or detergent and are used to control soft-bodied pests, such as aphids and whiteflies, by suffocating them.

Functions of Organic Sprays and Dusts

- Pest Control: Organic sprays and dusts are used to control pests, including insects, mites, and fungal diseases, by killing or deterring them from feeding on crops.
- **Disease Control:** Organic sprays and dusts can also be used to control plant diseases, such as powdery mildew and blackspot, by killing the fungal spores or inhibiting their growth.

Factors Influencing the Effectiveness

- **Timing:** The effectiveness of organic sprays and dusts can be influenced by the timing of their application. For example, applying them when pests are in their early stages of development can increase their effectiveness.

- **Weather:** Weather conditions, such as high humidity or heavy rainfall, can reduce the effectiveness of organic sprays and dusts by washing them off the plants or reducing their efficacy.

- **Pest Resistance:** Over time, pests can develop resistance to certain organic sprays and dusts, making them less effective.

- **Application Method:** The method of application, such as using a spray bottle or dust applicator, can influence the effectiveness of organic sprays and dusts.

Safety Considerations

While organic sprays and dusts are considered safer than chemical pesticides, they can still pose risks to human health and the environment if not used properly. Some common safety considerations include:

- **Skin and Eye Irritation:** Some organic sprays and dusts can cause skin and eye irritation, so it is important to wear protective clothing and goggles when applying them.

- **Toxicity to Beneficial Insects:** Some organic sprays and dusts can be toxic to beneficial insects, such as bees, so it is important to apply them at times when pollinators are not active.

- **Toxicity to Non-Target Species:** Some organic sprays and dusts can be toxic to non-target species, such as birds and beneficial insects, so it is important to follow label instructions and avoid spraying near water sources.

Natural Fertilizers

Natural fertilizers are organic materials that are used to provide essential nutrients to plants. Unlike synthetic fertilizers, which are made from chemicals, natural fertilizers are derived from plant and animal matter, minerals, and other organic sources. In this chapter, we will explore the different types of natural fertilizers, their functions, and the factors that influence their effectiveness.

Types of Natural Fertilizers

- **Animal Manures:** Animal manures, such as cow manure and chicken manure, are a rich source of nitrogen, phosphorus, and potassium, as well as other essential micronutrients.

- **Compost:** Compost is made from decomposed organic matter, such as kitchen waste, yard trimmings, and plant material, and is a rich source of nutrients and soil organic matter.

- **Rock Minerals:** Rock minerals, such as rock phosphate and granite meal, are slowly released into the soil and provide a long-term source of nutrients.

- **Green Manures:** Green manures are crops that are grown specifically for their ability to add organic matter and nutrients to the soil when they are incorporated into the soil.

Functions of Natural Fertilizers

Nutrient Supply: Natural fertilizers provide essential nutrients to plants, such as nitrogen, phosphorus, and potassium, to support their growth and development.

Soil Fertility: Natural fertilizers also help to improve soil fertility by increasing the organic matter content of the soil and promoting the activity of beneficial soil microorganisms.

Disease Suppression: Natural fertilizers can also help to suppress plant diseases by promoting the health and vitality of the plant, making it more resistant to disease.

Factors Influencing the Effectiveness of Natural Fertilizers

- **Soil Type:** The effectiveness of natural fertilizers can be influenced by the type of soil in which they are applied, as some soils may have low levels of certain nutrients or may be poorly suited to certain types of plants.

- **Weather:** Weather conditions, such as heavy rainfall or drought, can also affect the effectiveness of natural fertilizers by washing them away or preventing them from being absorbed by the plants.

- **Rate of Application:** The rate of application of natural fertilizers can also influence their effectiveness, as too much fertilizer can lead to nutrient imbalances or the release of harmful chemicals into the environment.

How to Fertilize Your Vegetable Garden

A well-fertilized garden will be able to produce a bountiful harvest, while an under-fertilized garden will result in poor growth and low yields. There are several techniques used to fertilize a garden, each of these has its own benefits and drawbacks, and it is important to understand them so that you can choose the best option for your garden. We have already seen the four main organic fertilizers; in the next few lines we will go into more detail on how to use them in practice to enhance your crop.

Animal Manures

Animal manures are a great source of nutrients for your garden. They are rich in nitrogen, phosphorus, and potassium, which are the three primary macronutrients that plants need to grow. Manures are also an excellent source of micronutrients, such as calcium and magnesium. Manures can be obtained from a variety of sources, including cows, horses, sheep, and chickens.

To use animal manures, simply spread them evenly over the soil and then till them into the soil to a depth of at least 8 inches. It is important to make sure that the manures are well-rotted before using them, as fresh manures can contain harmful bacteria that can be harmful to plants and people. Additionally, manures should be applied in the fall or winter, so that they have time to break down and be incorporated into the soil before planting season.

Compost

Compost is an excellent way to improve soil quality. It is made from a variety of organic materials, including leaves, grass clippings, fruit and vegetable scraps, and yard waste. As these materials decompose, they release nutrients into the soil, which are then absorbed by the plants. Compost also helps to improve soil structure and drainage, and it helps to reduce erosion.

To use compost, simply spread it over the soil in a layer about 2 inches thick. Then, till it into the soil to a depth of at least 8 inches. It is best to use compost in the fall or winter, so that it has time to break down and be incorporated into the soil before planting season.

Rock Minerals

Rock minerals are another great way to improve soil quality. They are made from ground up rock, such as granite or basalt, and are a source of essential micronutrients that plants need to grow. Rock minerals can be applied directly to the soil or mixed into compost or other fertilizers.

To use rock minerals, simply spread them evenly over the soil and then till them into the soil to a depth of at least 8 inches. It is best to use rock minerals in the fall or winter, so that they have time to break down and be incorporated into the soil before planting season.

Green Manures

Green manures are plants that are grown specifically for the purpose of improving soil quality. They are usually grown in between crops, and are then tilled into the soil to add organic matter and nutrients. Some of the most popular green manures include clover, alfalfa, and winter wheat.

To use green manures, simply plant the seeds in your garden and allow the plants to grow until they reach maturity. Then, till them into the soil to a depth of at least 8 inches. It is best to use green manures in the fall or winter, so that they have time to break down and be incorporated into the soil before planting season.

Natural Nutrient Value Chart

Material	% N	% P	% K
Sheep	0.6	0.33	0.75
Compost	1.5	0.5	1
Rock Phosphate	0	25	0
Fish Meal	10	4	0
Milorganite	5	2-5	2
Cow	0.25	0.15	0.25
Wood Ashes	0	1-2	3-7
Bone Meal	1	11	0
Swine	0.3	0.3	0.3
Poultry	2	2	1
Kelp	1	0,5	9
Peat & muck	1.5	0.25	0.5
Dried Blood	12	1.5	0.5
Urea	45	0	0
Horse	0.3	0.15	0.5

Sustainable Practices

Sustainable vegetable gardening refers to growing vegetables in an environmentally responsible manner that conserves natural resources and protects the environment. This approach seeks to maximize efficiency and minimize waste, while producing healthy and nutritious food. Some of the key practices involved in sustainable vegetable gardening include rainwater harvesting, greywater recycling, and permaculture design. These methods help to conserve water, reduce the use of chemical fertilizers and pesticides, and promote a healthier soil and ecosystem. By implementing these practices, gardeners can create a thriving and sustainable vegetable garden that provides delicious, nutritious produce while also supporting the health of the planet.

RAINWATER HARVESTING

This technique can provide a significant source of water for your garden and reduce the amount of water you need to draw from other sources, such as municipal water systems or wells. In this chapter, we will discuss the basics of rainwater harvesting and how you can implement it in your own vegetable garden.

Benefits of Rainwater Harvesting

Rainwater harvesting provides several benefits for vegetable gardening, including:

- Saving Water: By collecting and using rainwater for irrigation, you can significantly reduce the amount of water you need to draw from other sources, helping you conserve water and save money on your water bill.

- Improved Soil Quality: Rainwater is naturally pH-balanced and contains fewer minerals and salts compared to tap water, making it better for your soil and plants. Over time, using rainwater for irrigation can improve the quality of your soil and promote healthier plant growth.

- Increased Water Efficiency: Rainwater harvesting systems are designed to collect and store as much water as possible, helping you make the most of each rainfall.

Getting Started with Rainwater Harvesting

To get started with rainwater harvesting in your vegetable garden, you will need to follow these steps:

1. **Determine the Size of Your System:** To determine the size of your rainwater harvesting system, you will need to consider the size of your garden and the amount of rainfall you receive each year. A larger garden will require a larger system, while a smaller garden can use a smaller system.

2. **Choose a Collection System:** There are several different types of collection systems you can use to collect rainwater, including gutter systems, barrel systems, and underground cisterns. Each system has its own advantages and disadvantages, so choose the one that best suits your needs and budget.

3. **Install the Collection System:** Once you have chosen a collection system, you will need to install it on your property. This may require the help of a professional, so be sure to research the installation process before you begin.

4. **Store the Rainwater:** Once you have collected the rainwater, you will need to store it in a tank or cistern. Make sure to choose a tank or cistern that is large enough to store the amount of water you need for your garden.

5. **Use the Rainwater for Irrigation:** Once you have collected and stored the rainwater, you can use it for irrigation purposes. Depending on the size of your system, you may need to use a pump to move the water from the tank or cistern to your garden.

Maintenance of Rainwater Harvesting Systems

To ensure that your rainwater harvesting system is working efficiently, you will need to perform regular maintenance. This may include cleaning gutters and downspouts, checking for leaks, and checking the water level in the tank or cistern. Regular maintenance will help you avoid problems and ensure that your system is working correctly. With the right collection system, storage tank or cistern, and regular maintenance, you can easily implement rainwater harvesting in your own vegetable garden and make the most of each rainfall.

Greywater Recycling

Greywater recycling is a sustainable and cost-effective way of using household wastewater for irrigation purposes. This water can come from sources such as shower drains, bathtubs, and sink drains, but not from toilets or kitchen sinks. By using this water in the garden, you can conserve water and reduce the demand for municipal water supplies.

Step-by-Step Guide to Greywater Recycling

1. Determine the source of the greywater. It's important to know what types of soaps and cleaners are used in the water source, as some may contain harmful chemicals that can harm plants.

2. Plan the greywater system. Decide how you want to transport the greywater to your garden. There are several options, such as gravity-fed systems, pump-fed systems, or even bucket-carrying.

3. Install the greywater system. It's important to follow local codes and regulations when installing a greywater system. Consider hiring a professional to ensure the system is properly installed.

4. Choose the right plants. Some plants are more tolerant to greywater than others. Choose plants that are drought-tolerant and can handle a higher salt content.

5. Irrigate the garden. Greywater should be used within 24 hours of being generated, and should be used on non-edible plants before edible crops.

6. Monitor the system. Regularly check for leaks and clogs, and make sure the water is being distributed evenly throughout the garden.

Benefits of Greywater Recycling

- Conserves water. Greywater recycling helps conserve water by using household wastewater for irrigation, reducing the demand for municipal water supplies.

- Reduces water bills. By using greywater for irrigation, you can reduce your monthly water bill.

- Helps the environment. Greywater recycling is an environmentally-friendly practice that reduces the amount of water that goes into septic systems and sewage treatment plants.

- Improves soil health. Greywater can add important nutrients to the soil, which can improve soil health and support the growth of healthy plants.

Overall, greywater recycling is a sustainable and cost-effective way to conserve water and support the growth of healthy vegetable gardens. By following these steps, you can successfully implement a greywater recycling system in your own garden.

Permaculture Design

Permaculture design is a holistic approach to gardening that incorporates sustainable and regenerative practices. This method involves creating a closed-loop system where resources are conserved and waste is transformed into new resources. Permaculture design is becoming increasingly popular among vegetable gardeners who want to grow food in an environmentally-friendly and self-sustaining way.

The Principles of Permaculture Design

Permaculture design is based on a set of principles that guide the way in which the garden is designed and managed. These principles include:

- Observe and interact: Observing and interacting with the natural systems in the garden allows gardeners to understand the patterns of nature and use them to their advantage.

- Catch and store energy: This principle involves capturing resources such as sunlight, water, and nutrients and storing them in the garden so they can be used when needed.

- Obtain a yield: This principle is about obtaining a yield from the garden that is both sustainable and regenerative. This means that the garden should produce food while also improving the health of the soil and other natural systems.

- Apply self-regulation and accept feedback: Self-regulation and accepting feedback are important principles in permaculture design because they allow gardeners to adjust their practices based on the results they see in the garden.

- Use and value diversity: Diversity is important in permaculture design because it creates a more resilient and stable system. This means incorporating a variety of crops, plants, and animals into the garden.

- Use edges and value the marginal: Edges are areas in the garden where two different ecosystems meet. In permaculture design, these areas are used to create new opportunities and increase productivity.
- Creatively use and respond to change: Change is inevitable in the garden, and permaculture design encourages gardeners to be creative and adapt to changes in their environment.

How to Apply Permaculture Design

Applying permaculture design to a vegetable garden involves creating a closed-loop system where resources are conserved and waste is transformed into new resources. This can be done by incorporating the following practices into the garden:

- Companion planting: Companion planting involves planting crops together that benefit each other. For example, planting beans and corn together can help fix nitrogen in the soil and provide support for the corn.
- Intercropping: Intercropping involves planting crops in close proximity to each other that have different growth habits. This helps to maximize space and reduce the impact of pests and diseases.
- Mulching: Mulching involves covering the soil with a layer of organic matter such as leaves, straw, or grass clippings. This helps to conserve moisture and improve soil health.
- Vermicomposting: Vermicomposting involves using worms to break down organic matter into compost. This compost can then be used to improve soil health and fertility.
- Rainwater harvesting: Collecting and storing rainwater for use in the garden is an important aspect of permaculture design. This helps to conserve water and reduce the need for irrigation.
- Greywater recycling: Recycling greywater (wastewater from household activities such as washing dishes or clothes) is a way to conserve water and reduce the amount of water that needs to be purified for use in the garden.
- Use of natural pest control: In permaculture design, natural pest control methods are used to maintain a healthy and thriving vegetable garden without relying on harmful chemicals.

Conclusion

Organic gardening is not only good for the environment, but it is also good for you, providing you with fresh, healthy produce that is free from harmful chemicals. By choosing to garden organically, you are taking an important step towards a more sustainable and environmentally friendly future. So if you are ready to start your own organic vegetable garden, grab your gloves and get started! With patience, persistence, and a little bit of know-how, you will soon be harvesting your own delicious, organic produce and enjoying all the benefits that come with it.

BOOK 3:

Growing Vegetable in Container

Introduction

Growing vegetables in containers is a convenient and rewarding way to produce your own fresh, healthy produce, regardless of the size of your outdoor space. Container gardening is perfect for those with limited garden space, apartment dwellers, or anyone who wants to enjoy the benefits of gardening without the hassle of maintaining a large garden plot.

In this book, you will learn everything you need to know about growing vegetables in containers, from selecting the right containers and soil to choosing the best plants for your climate and space. You will discover the ins and outs of container gardening, including how to provide the right amount of light, water, and nutrients for your plants to thrive.

The Benefits of Container Gardening

Container gardening is a popular and growing trend for urban and suburban gardeners alike. Container gardening involves growing plants in pots or containers instead of directly in the ground. Container gardening has several benefits over traditional in-ground gardening, making it a great option for those who want to grow plants in small spaces or have limited mobility. Let's see all the benefits:

- **Flexibility:** Container gardening allows you to move your plants around your property to take advantage of the best growing conditions, or even bring them indoors during inclement weather.

- **Space-saving:** Container gardening is ideal for small yards, balconies, patios, or decks where there may not be enough space for a traditional garden.

- **Soil quality control:** Container gardening allows you to control the quality of the soil, ensuring that your plants have the right nutrients and drainage to grow strong and healthy.

- **Pest and disease control:** Growing plants in containers can help limit the spread of pests and diseases, as well as make it easier to treat any issues that do arise.

- **Improved accessibility:** Container gardening is a great option for people with limited mobility, as it allows them to garden at a height that is comfortable for them.

- **Enhanced aesthetics:** Container gardening provides an opportunity to add color, texture, and interest to your outdoor spaces. By selecting plants that complement each other and arranging them creatively, you can create a beautiful and personalized outdoor area.

- **Increased yields:** Container gardening can result in higher yields compared to in-ground gardening, as containers warm up faster in the spring and stay warm longer in the fall, extending the growing season.

- **Water conservation:** Container gardening allows you to conserve water, as you can control the amount of water your plants receive and prevent water from being lost to evaporation or runoff.

Container Selection and Preparation

How do I choose which container to use? Here are some tips on how to choose the best pots for plants and flowers or for growing a vegetable garden on the balcony, pros and cons of the containers that are used for growing in the garden, on the terrace or inside the house. In the next few lines we focus on the choice of pots and boxes, a decision that should be guided by the concepts of efficiency and practicality rather than just imagination and personal taste.

DIMENSION

Pots for growing a vegetable garden on the balcony should not be too small: to ensure good yields and to anchor themselves firmly in the soil, the roots of vegetables need a sufficient amount of soil. If you choose dwarf plants such as mini eggplants or mini tomatoes, you will certainly need less space and do not have to employ large plastic pots.

On the other hand, however, you should also not choose pots that are too large because dangerous moisture buildup can form in the part of the soil not reached by the roots, which is ideal for mold and pests.

Regarding the depth of the pot: in general, it should never be less than 25 cm because even aromatic plants, which adapt easily in any situation, would have something to say about it. For salads, radishes and other vegetables that have short roots, shallow boxes are suitable, while for vegetables that need to develop the root system in depth, such as tomatoes, cucumbers, eggplant, and zucchini, containers at least 35 centimeters deep are needed.

POT SHAPE

You can choose square or round garden pots. In general, plant pots are conical or bowl-shaped, while outdoor planters also have fancier shapes accompanied by side pockets to match different flowers and plants. There is also the corner vase. If you opt for the rectangular or square vase:

- **PRO:** Rectangular containers can be placed side by side. So they allow you to take up less space or save useful space if you grow a vegetable garden on the balcony
- **CON:** Balcony pots are often round. These allow groupings that are more aesthetically pleasing but clearly the sides do not stay together and therefore you will not have optimal space utilization.

Design is part of this object. There are modern plant pots or the more classic ones. Some are designed for kitchen and aromatic plants rather than magnetic for small pots.

MATERIALS

Commercially, there are pots and planters made of many materials. Outdoor pots made of terracotta are the most classic, but you can also find ones made of sophisticated fiberglass, a common plastic, wood, cast iron, grés or ceramic etc.

One criterion for choosing is definitely aesthetics but also practicality and functionality: these materials are not equivalent and even here there are pros and cons. *So how to choose the most suitable vase materials?*

Plastic planters

There are many plastic pots or planters made of plastic, because it is a very common material and easy to produce. They are the classic indoor pots that many of us use. It also allows for large pots that remain very practical.

- **PRO:** Plastic plant pots are the most popular. They are sturdy and weatherproof, so they last a long time, and they are lightweight and easy to move. They are inexpensive outdoor pots because they cost little, and in summer they retain soil moisture better because their walls are waterproof
- **CON:** Plastic pots do not allow good air circulation in the soil and they are also not aesthetically pleasing. Also keep in mind that with the high temperatures from prolonged exposure to the sun, especially if they are dark in color, they get very hot and there is a danger that they will burn the roots

Be careful not to overwater so as not to cause water stagnation in the plastic pot. Also, if you use outdoor plastic pots, rain may stagnate in the saucer, be careful! This material is also used in the production of plastic flower pots, as it is suitable for all these characteristics.

Terracotta pots

Terracotta garden pots are common. They vary in size; it is not difficult to find small terracotta pots on the market. In general:

- **PRO:** Terracotta pots are resistant to heat and frost, without cracking. They are porous and therefore allow both the soil and the plant roots to breathe. Their weight provides stability which is good especially if your terrace is exposed to gusts of wind
- **CON:** Because they are porous they allow water to evaporate quickly, so you will have to water your plants more frequently during the summer. However, their weight does not allow you to move them easily and they are fragile at the slightest bump. They also command higher prices, which is why you can also find them used. Large terracotta pots are expensive and heavy once filled with soil but they sure look great!

Thus, balcony planters are a great solution in terracotta although it is preferable to anchor them to a support to prevent them from falling down below!

Wooden pots

Wooden pots are another solution to consider. For example, many people try their hand at DIY wooden pots because they have good dexterity and inventiveness.

- **PRO:** Wood is also a great material because it is porous, which allows air and water to circulate between the fibers and between the cracks in the laths. It also does not overheat in the sun allowing the soil to maintain freshness and moisture even in the hottest months
- **CON:** Wooden containers are rather expensive and deteriorate, depending on the wood they are made from, in a rather rapid time frame

To prevent wooden garden pots from deteriorating, some models have an internal galvanized sheet metal tub, which in contrast negates the benefit of the wood's porosity.

DRAINAGE

Balcony pots as well as garden pots or indoor planters have a common denominator that you must pay attention to drainage! Each container must have one or more holes at the base to allow excess water, whether rainwater or water from manual or automatic irrigation, to drain away. This will prevent stagnation that can be fatal to the roots by causing rot and mold.

Additional tip: If your pots do not have these holes, simply make them with a drill.

Saucer

This chapter would not be complete if it did not discuss a fundamental element of every plant pot: the saucer. A saucer must be placed under each pot to collect excess water that the plant will then slowly absorb.

In addition, to promote water runoff from under the pots, larger boxes and containers should be raised slightly off the floor by resting them on pieces of stone or brick. We recommend that these supports be placed in a way that does not affect the stability of the pot. You can also find ceramic or terracotta supports on the market specifically designed for this purpose.

Do you have a large, heavy pot? Resort to a saucer with wheels: thanks to the wheels you can move it more easily. There is the rectangular or square saucer, in many materials (plastic saucers remain an excellent practical and inexpensive solution) as well as ceramic, in all colors starting with white. Which one do you prefer?

Additional tip: If the water in the saucer stands too long, for example rainwater, it is better to suck it up with special hand pumps to avoid stagnation.

As written earlier, there is no such thing as an ideal pot, but our intent is to provide helpful hints and guidance for making the best choices. It depends on what you grow, where and how green your thumb is! We hope the pros and cons laid out will be useful to those reading, and we await cues from the more unusual solutions. We for example have made a chair pot or happened to see aromatics grown in hiking boots!

VEGETABLE CONTAINER GARDENING CHART GUIDE

Vegetable Plant	Minimum Container Size	Light Requirement	Space Between Plants
Peas	2-5 gallon	Full Sun / Partial Shade	3-4 inches
Peas, Snow	2-5 gallon	Full Sun / Partial Shade	3-4 inches
Arugula	1/2 gallon	Full Sun / Partial Shade	3-4 inches
Beets	1/2 gallon	Full Sun / Partial Shade	2-3 inches
Chard, Swiss	1/2 gallon	Full Sun / Partial Shade	4-6 inches
Lettuce, Leaf	1/2 gallon	Full Sun / Partial Shade	4-6 inches
Onions, Green	1/2 gallon	Full Sun / Partial Shade	2-3 inches
Carrots	1 quart	Full Sun / Partial Shade	2-3 inches
Radishes	1 Pint	Full Sun / Partial Shade	1 Plant per container
Tomato, Cherry	1 gallon	Full Sun	1 Plant per container
Turnips	1 gallon	Full Sun	2-3 inches
Beans, Bush	2 gallon	Full Sun	2-3 inches
Peppers, Bell	2 gallon	Full Sun	1 Plant per container
Beans, Pole	5 gallon	Full Sun	2-4 inches
Broccoli	5 gallon	Full Sun	12-18 inches
Cabbage	5 gallon	Full Sun / Partial Shade	12-18 inches
Collards	5 gallon	Full Sun	5-7 Inches
Cucumbers	5 gallon	Full Sun	14-18 inches
Eggplant	5 gallon	Full Sun	1 Plant per container
Kale	5 gallon	Full Sun / Partial Shade	10-15 inches
Peppers, Hot	5 gallon	Full Sun	1-2 Plant per container
Squash	5 gallon	Full Sun	1 Plant per container
Tomato	5 gallon	Full Sun	1 Plant per container
Zucchini	5 gallon	Full Sun	1 Plant per container

Common Vegetables & How to Grow Them

TOMATOES

Ideal Temperature: Tomatoes prefer warm weather and an ideal temperature range is between 60°F to 85°F.

Amount of Water Required: Tomatoes require consistent moisture and it is recommended to water the plants deeply once a week or more frequently in hot weather. It is important to avoid overwatering and to allow the soil to dry out a bit between waterings.

Expected Yield: On average, a healthy tomato plant can produce up to 10 to 20 pounds of fruit per growing season. The actual yield may vary based on the variety and growing conditions.

Main Problem: The main problem with growing tomatoes in pots is the potential for limited root growth and the need for proper support. It is important to provide adequate support for the plant as it grows and to prune it as necessary to promote healthy growth.

Ideal Pot: A 5-gallon container is ideal for growing a single tomato plant. Make sure the pot has good drainage and is at least 24 inches in diameter and 18 inches deep to allow proper root growth.

PEPPERS

Ideal temperature: Peppers prefer warm temperatures between 70°F to 85°F. They do not tolerate frost and should not be planted outside until all danger of frost has passed.

Amount of water required: Peppers need consistent moisture, but not waterlogged soil. Water the plants deeply once a week or when the top inch of the soil feels dry to the touch.

Expected yield: A single pepper plant can produce 10 to 20 peppers per season. The exact yield will depend on the variety of pepper, the growing conditions, and the care provided.

Main problem: The main problem with growing peppers in pots is keeping the soil moist. Overwatering can lead to root rot, while underwatering can cause the plant to wilt and drop its fruit.

Ideal pot: Peppers need a large pot with good drainage. A pot that is at least 12-18 inches in diameter and 12-18 inches deep is ideal for a single pepper plant. Terra cotta pots are a good choice as they allow the soil to breathe, but any type of pot that is large enough and has drainage holes will work.

LETTUCE

Ideal temperature: Lettuce grows best in cool temperatures between 45°F and 75°F. Avoid planting during the hottest part of the day as this can cause the leaves to bolt (grow tall and produce seeds) quickly.

Amount of water required: Lettuce plants need to be kept consistently moist. Water the soil deeply whenever the top inch of the soil is dry. Avoid letting the soil dry out completely, or the plants will become stunted and bitter.

Expected yield: A single lettuce plant can produce several harvests of leaves over several weeks. You can expect to harvest about 4-6 ounces of greens per plant.

Main problem: The most common problem with growing lettuce in pots is bolting, which can be caused by hot temperatures, low moisture, or long days. To prevent bolting, grow lettuce in a cool, shady spot, water regularly, and avoid planting lettuce varieties that are known to bolt quickly.

Ideal pot: Lettuce plants are shallow rooted and do not need a lot of soil depth, so a pot that is at least 6-8 inches deep and 8-10 inches in diameter will work well. You can also grow lettuce in a larger pot and harvest the outer leaves, leaving the inner leaves to continue growing.

SPINACH

Ideal temperature: Spinach grows best in cool weather, with temperatures ranging between 40-70°F (4-21°C).

Amount of water required: Spinach requires consistent moisture to grow, but be careful not to overwater as this can lead to root rot. It is recommended to water spinach once or twice a week, providing enough water to keep the soil evenly moist but not waterlogged.

Expected yield: One spinach plant can produce a yield of 4-6 ounces of fresh spinach leaves.

Main problem: One of the main problems with growing spinach in pots is that it bolts (goes to seed) quickly in warm temperatures, so it's important to plant it in cooler weather or in a shaded area. Additionally, spinach is also susceptible to leaf spots and downy mildew, so it's important to keep the foliage dry and practice good air circulation to prevent these diseases.

Ideal pot: Spinach can be grown in any type of container with adequate drainages, such as a 5-gallon pot or a grow bag, at least 8-10 inches in diameter and 6-8 inches deep. Make sure to choose a container that is large enough to accommodate the plant's root system and allow for proper drainage.

CUCUMBERS

Ideal Temperature: Cucumbers prefer warm temperatures and grow best in temperatures between 70-85°F. They are a warm-season crop and can be damaged by temperatures below 50°F.

Amount of Water Required: Cucumbers are heavy drinkers and require regular watering, especially when they are fruiting. The soil should be kept consistently moist, but not waterlogged. It is important to avoid letting the soil dry out completely as this can cause stunted growth and poor yields.

Expected Yield: One cucumber plant grown in a pot can yield several cucumbers throughout the growing season. The size of the pot will affect the yield, but a 5-gallon pot is a good size for growing one plant.

Main Problem: Cucumbers are prone to several pest and disease issues, including powdery mildew, aphids, and cucumber beetles. These problems can be controlled through regular monitoring and proper garden maintenance.

Ideal Pot: Cucumbers are a climbing plant and will require a larger pot for support. A 5-gallon or larger pot is recommended for growing cucumbers in pots. The pot should also have good drainage and be made of a material that will retain moisture and provide good aeration, such as terra cotta or plastic.

ZUCCHINI

Ideal Temperature: Zucchini plants prefer warm temperatures, between 65-85°F. When temperatures go above 90°F, the plant's growth can slow down or stop completely.

Amount of Water Required: Zucchini plants need to be kept consistently moist, but not waterlogged. You should aim to water your plants 1-2 times a week, making sure to give the soil a good soak each time. If the temperature is particularly hot, you may need to water more frequently.

Expected Yield: One mature zucchini plant can produce anywhere from 2-10 zucchini, depending on the variety and growing conditions.

Main Problem: The most common problems with growing zucchini in pots include powdery mildew, poor pollination, and over-watering. To avoid these problems, make sure to choose a pot with good drainage and avoid getting water on the leaves when watering.

Ideal Pot: Zucchini plants have a large root system and grow quickly, so they need a large pot. Choose a pot that is at least 12 inches deep and 18 inches in diameter. This will give your plant enough space to grow and will allow for good drainage. Additionally, make sure the pot has multiple drainage holes at the bottom to prevent waterlogging.

CARROTS

Ideal Temperature: Carrots prefer a cooler climate and grow best in temperatures between 55-75°F (13-24°C). If temperatures get too high, the growth of the carrots may become stunted and the flavor may be affected.

Amount of Water Required: Carrots require a consistent water supply to grow properly. It is important to keep the soil evenly moist but not waterlogged. Over-watering can cause the roots to rot, so make sure to let the top inch of soil dry out between waterings.

Expected Yield: Each carrot plant can produce up to 1-2 pounds of carrots per season, depending on the size of the pot.

Main Problem: Carrots can be susceptible to pests such as root maggots, aphids, and cutworms. It is important to monitor the plants regularly and take measures to control these pests as needed.

Ideal Pot: Carrots prefer a deep pot, at least 12 inches in depth, with good drainage. A 5-gallon pot is suitable for growing 2-3 carrot plants. The pot should be made of a material that retains moisture, such as terra cotta, to help maintain a consistent soil moisture level.

RADISHES

Ideal Temperature: Radishes prefer a cool growing environment and do well in temperatures ranging from 45-75°F. They are a cool-season crop and can be grown in spring or fall when the weather is cooler.

Amount of Water Required: Radishes need to be kept consistently moist and should be watered regularly, but not over watered as this can cause them to split. It is best to water the soil directly, keeping the leaves dry to avoid fungal diseases.

Amount of Crop to Expect: Depending on the variety, each radish plant can produce several radishes. A good rule of thumb is to allow 2-3 inches (5-7 cm) between each plant when planting.

Main Problem with the Plant: Radishes are generally a low-maintenance crop, but they can be prone to problems such as stunted growth, split radishes, and insect pests like aphids.

Ideal Pot: Radishes are small and do well in shallow containers. Choose a pot that is at least 6 inches deep and has adequate drainage holes. A 12-inch diameter pot can accommodate 4-6 radish plants.

BEETS

Ideal temperature: Beets prefer cool temperatures between 50-65°F (10-18°C). They can tolerate temperatures up to 75°F (24°C) but will grow slower.

Amount of water required: Beets need a consistent amount of water to prevent the roots from becoming tough and woody. Aim to keep the soil consistently moist, but not waterlogged. It's best to water your beets at the base of the plant, avoiding getting water on the leaves.

Crop yield: Each beet plant can produce multiple beets, but the exact yield will depend on the size of your pot and the growing conditions. A 5-gallon pot can comfortably accommodate 2-3 beet plants, and you can expect to harvest 3-4 beets per plant.

Main problem: Beet greens are susceptible to flea beetles, which can cause holes in the leaves. Covering the pots with row covers can help prevent damage. Another common problem is root maggots, which can damage the roots. To prevent this, rotate your crops and avoid planting beets in the same location year after year.

Ideal pot: Choose a container that is at least 10-12 inches deep and 12-14 inches in diameter, with good drainage holes. A larger pot will allow room for multiple plants and will also help to prevent the soil from drying out too quickly. Be sure to use a good quality potting soil mix, or a mixture of equal parts garden soil, compost, and perlite.

Container Gardening Techniques

When we think of gardening in pots or similar containers, people who live in the city in apartments immediately come to mind. But if you reflect further, growing plants in pots is suitable for anyone, even those who own a garden of any size. To start container gardening, it's important to understand the three essential elements that will determine the success of your plants: soil, irrigation, and fertilizers.

Soil: The type of soil you use in your containers is critical to the health of your plants. When choosing soil, look for a high-quality potting mix that is specifically designed for container gardening. This type of soil contains the right balance of nutrients and structure to ensure good drainage and aeration.

Irrigation: Container plants are vulnerable to drying out quickly, so consistent watering is essential. To avoid over-watering, make sure that your container has good drainage holes and that you water your plants deeply, but not too frequently.

Fertilizers: Container plants often require more fertilization than plants grown in the ground, as they're confined to a limited volume of soil. To ensure that your plants receive the nutrients they need, use a balanced fertilizer and follow the manufacturer's instructions for application.

With the right soil, irrigation, and fertilization, your container gardening journey is sure to be a success. So, let's get started, and grow some delicious and healthy food!

THE IDEAL POTTING SOIL

Soil is one of the most important components of container gardening, as it provides the structure and nutrients for your plants to grow. The right soil helps the plants to grow healthy, and strong and produce a bountiful harvest. If the soil is poor in quality, it can lead to poor plant growth, low yields and a host of other problems. Hence, it is important to choose the right soil for your container vegetable garden.

When it comes to container vegetable gardening, the soil needs to have several key characteristics to ensure the plants grow well. The soil should be well-draining, yet retain enough moisture to keep the plants hydrated. It should also be rich in nutrients and have a good balance of organic matter, air, and water. A soil pH of 6.0 to 6.8 is ideal for most vegetables.

If you are looking to make your own soil mix for container vegetable gardening, you can start by using a base of peat moss or coir, which helps to improve the soil structure and water-holding capacity. To this, you can add vermiculite or perlite to improve drainage, and compost or well-rotted manure to add organic matter and nutrients. A recipe for a basic soil mix for container vegetable gardening could look like this:

Ingredients:

- 2 parts peat moss or coir
- 2 parts vermiculite or perlite
- 1 part compost or well-rotted manure

Instructions:

1. Start by mixing the peat moss or coir with the vermiculite or perlite in a large container.
2. Add the compost or well-rotted manure to the mix and stir thoroughly.
3. Store the soil mix in a dry, cool place until you are ready to use it.

It is important to note that different vegetables have different soil requirements, so be sure to research the specific needs of the plants you plan to grow. Another option is to use pre-made soil mixes specifically designed for container vegetable gardening. These mixes can be found at most garden centers and come ready to use, saving you the time and effort of making your own mix. However, it is important to read the label carefully to ensure that the mix is suitable for the types of vegetables you plan to grow.

THE PROPER WATERING TECHNIQUE

The proper amount and frequency of watering are essential to ensure the health and growth of your plants. In this section, we will cover the basics of appropriate watering in container gardening and provide tips on figuring out when to water your plants, as well as suggestions and common problems to avoid.

How & When to Water

When watering your container garden, it is important to avoid overhead watering, which can cause water to splash onto the leaves and create a conducive environment for diseases and pests. Instead, water at the base of the plants, making sure the water soaks deeply into the soil.

One way to determine when to water your container garden is by feeling the soil. When the top inch of soil is dry, it is time to water. Another way to check the moisture level is to insert a finger into the soil. If the soil feels dry up to the second knuckle, it is time to water.

Tips:

- Water in the morning or early afternoon, allowing the soil to dry out before nightfall. This will help prevent fungal diseases.
- Water slowly and deeply, so the water has a chance to soak into the soil and reach the roots.
- Avoid watering too frequently, as this can cause root rot.
- Make sure the container has adequate drainage to allow excess water to drain out.

Common Problems to Avoid:

- Overwatering: Overwatering can cause root rot and prevent the plant from getting the oxygen it needs to survive.
- Underwatering: If a plant does not receive enough water, its leaves will wilt, and it may become stunted or die.
- Inconsistent watering: Inconsistent watering can stress a plant and prevent it from growing properly.

FERTILIZATION

Fertilization is a key aspect of container gardening. The right type and amount of fertilizer can provide plants with the necessary nutrients for growth and production, while avoiding common problems such as fertilizer burn. In the next few lines, we will discuss the various types of fertilizers available for container gardening, how often to apply them, and how much to use them.

Types of Fertilizers:

Organic Fertilizers: Organic fertilizers come from natural sources and are usually derived from plant or animal materials. They are slow-release, meaning that they release nutrients over a longer period of time, providing a steady source of nutrition for plants. Examples of organic fertilizers include compost, bone meal, blood meal, and fish emulsion.

Chemical Fertilizers: These are synthetic and are available in a wide range of formulations. They can provide plants with quick and concentrated doses of nutrients. However, they can also have negative impacts on the soil, such as reducing soil life and increasing soil salinity.

Slow-release Fertilizers: These are chemical fertilizers that are formulated to release their nutrients slowly over time. They provide a continuous supply of nutrients to the plants, reducing the need for frequent applications.

Complete Fertilizers: Complete fertilizers contain all three essential nutrients *(nitrogen, phosphorus, and potassium)* in balanced amounts. They are a good choice for container gardens because they provide a balanced diet for plants.

Specialty Fertilizers: Specialty fertilizers are designed for specific types of plants and their unique needs. For example, tomato plants require a high amount of calcium, so there is a fertilizer available specifically for them that provides this nutrient.

Frequency of Fertilization

The frequency of fertilization depends on a variety of factors, including the type of fertilizer used, the stage of growth of the plants, and the weather conditions. A general rule of thumb is to apply fertilizer every 4 to 6 weeks during the growing season. If you are using organic fertilizers, it is best to apply them at the beginning of the growing season and then every 4 to 6 weeks after that. Chemical fertilizers can be applied every 2 to 4 weeks during the growing season.

Amount of Fertilizer

The amount of fertilizer to use depends on the type of fertilizer you are using, the stage of growth of the plants, and the size of the containers. Generally, it is best to follow the manufacturer's recommendations for application rates. However, if you are using organic fertilizers, it is best to apply them in moderation, as they can lead to fertilizer burn if applied in excess.

Seeds or Cuttings?

Starting a garden from seeds or cuttings is a common and fulfilling way to grow new plants. Both methods have their own pros and cons and it is important to understand them in order to make the best decision for your garden. In this chapter, we will discuss the benefits and drawbacks of each method, provide instructions for starting seeds and cuttings, and explain when each method is best used.

STARTING FROM SEEDS: PROS AND CONS

PROS:

- **Cost-effective:** Starting from seeds is often less expensive than buying young plants or cuttings.

- **Wide variety:** Seeds are readily available and come in a huge variety of species, giving you a broad range of options to choose from.

- **Early start:** Starting seeds indoors allows you to get a head start on the growing season, especially in areas with harsh winters.

CONS:

- **Time-consuming:** Starting seeds can be a time-consuming process, requiring patience and attention to detail.

- **Requires equipment:** Starting seeds requires equipment such as containers, soil, and grow lights, which can add to the initial cost of starting a garden from seeds.

- **Risk of failure:** There is a risk of failure when starting from seeds, as some may not germinate, or the plants may not grow as expected.

Instructions for Starting from Seeds

1. Choose the right containers: Fill seed trays or pots with a seed-starting mix, making sure to moisten the soil before planting.

2. Sow seeds: Sow seeds according to the packet instructions, making sure to plant at the appropriate depth and spacing.

3. Provide light and moisture: Place the containers in a warm, bright area and keep the soil moist. A grow light can be used to provide extra light if necessary.

4. Keep soil warm: Some seeds require warm soil to germinate, so use a heating mat if necessary.

5. Thin out seedlings: Once the seeds have germinated and the seedlings have emerged, thin out the weaker ones to give the stronger seedlings room to grow.

6. Transplant: Once the seedlings are big enough, transplant them into larger containers or into the ground.

Best Time of Year for Starting from Seeds

The best time to start seeds depends on the type of plant you want to grow and the climate in your area. In general, seeds for warm-season crops, such as tomatoes and peppers, should be started indoors about 6-8 weeks before the last expected frost. Seeds for cool-season crops, such as lettuce and spinach, can be started indoors about 4-6 weeks before the last expected frost.

Starting from Cuttings: Pros and Cons

PROS:

- **Faster growth:** Cuttings root more quickly than seeds and produce plants that are identical to the parent plant.

- **Reliable:** Starting from cuttings eliminates the risk of failure associated with starting from seeds.

- **Reduced cost:** Cuttings are often cheaper than buying young plants.

CONS:

- **Limited variety:** Cuttings are only available for a limited range of plant species.

- **Requires parent plant:** To start a cutting, you need to have access to a healthy parent plant.

Instructions for Starting from Cuttings

1. Choose the right cuttings: Take cuttings from healthy, non-flowering shoots and make sure to remove any leaves from the bottom 2-3 inches of the cutting.

2. Prepare the cutting: Dip the cut end of the cutting in rooting hormone, then insert it into a container filled with rooting mix.

3. Provide moisture and light: Cover the container with a plastic bag to create a greenhouse effect and place it in a bright but not direct light. Keep the soil moist.

4. Monitor rooting: Check the cuttings regularly for root development, usually after 2-3 weeks. Once roots have formed, remove the plastic bag.

5. Transplant: Once the cuttings have been rooted, transplant them into larger containers or into the ground.

Best Time of Year for Starting from Cuttings

The best time to start cuttings depends on the type of plant you want to grow and the climate in your area. In general, cuttings should be taken during the growing season when the parent plant is actively growing.

Starting a garden from seeds or cuttings is a great way to grow new plants. Both methods have their own pros and cons, and it is important to understand them in order to make the best decision for your garden. Whether you choose to start from seeds or cuttings, the key to success is proper preparation, attention to detail, and patience. Happy gardening!

Troubleshooting & Problem-Solving

Even when you are certain that you are providing your plant with everything it needs, there is frequently some error you miss. Most blunders are the result of over-caring for your plant, even when it is not necessarily required for its health. In order to prevent unintentionally causing harm to your plants, it is vital to understand what is easy to get wrong when caring for potted plants. Let's look at the top 5 mistakes you make with your potted plants together!

Problem #1: Getting plants that are not suitable for your space

The first and most frequent error made by novice vegetable gardeners is this one. It is crucial to consider your children's health right away, i.e., when you begin selecting the varieties of veggies to bring into your home.

For instance, picking a plant that requires eight hours of sunlight and placing it in a north-facing home that only receives the morning light is already a setback. Always conduct some study before purchasing a plant and consider how much light it needs. *How many hours of light are available in my home instead? Is a lot of moisture required? Can I put it inside the home or on the balcony?*

If you can at least fulfill these prerequisites, you'll see that you'll get off to a terrific start!

Problem #2: Giving too much care to your veggies

I can appreciate how exciting it is to have new vegetables to tend to since they provide joy to your daily life and you want to do your best to provide them with everything they require to flourish. However, it's crucial to avoid going overboard because giving your plant too much care will stress it out unnecessarily.

Try to satisfy the plant's needs whenever possible because the risk is that you will over-fertilize, over-water, or expose it to too much sunshine, which will cause its leaves to burn.

Problem #3: Improper watering

Both watering too much and not watering at all can be detrimental behaviors to the health of your vegetables and can cause irreversible damage.

Understanding when and how much water to give your houseplant is important. The general rule is that if you stick your finger into the top 2-3 inches of soil and the soil is completely dry, it is time to give your plant a drink. If the soil is damp, don't water it: give the plant a few more days before checking again.

Problem #4: Too low moisture

As we slather moisturizer lotion on our skin in winter, we tend to forget that plants also like a little extra moisture. We also fail to remember that plants like humidity levels between 45 and 55 percent, which means that even when they receive adequate watering, their leaves can dry up.

They will adore the humidity you generate around your aquarium if you have one. If not, think about investing in a humidifier or placing a saucer under the plant pot filled with water and expanded clay pebbles to maintain a healthy level of humidity.

Problem #5: Improper use of pots

Using pots the wrong way is the quickest way for roots to rot. Make sure your vegetables are grown in a planter or pot with drainage holes in the bottom.

This will ensure that your plant's roots do not rest in soggy wet soil. If the decorative planter cover you have chosen to pendant with your décor does not have drainage holes, I recommend that you simply place the plant with the plastic nursery pot inside the planter cover.

That way, you can remove the plant from its nursery pot by simply lifting it out of the decorative pot to water it and letting the excess water runoff before putting it back in the decorative pot. NEVER allow water to pool in the pot cover; it is lethal to the plant.

Conclusion

Container gardening is a fantastic way to bring the joys of gardening into your home, regardless of the size of your space. With the right choice of plants and containers, you can create a thriving garden on your balcony, patio, or windowsill. The key to success in container gardening is to understand the specific needs of your plants and to provide them with the right combination of light, water, and soil. With proper care and attention, you can create a garden that is not only beautiful but also provides you with fresh, healthy food.

This book has provided you with a comprehensive guide to container gardening, from the basics of selecting plants and containers to the more advanced techniques for growing and caring for your garden. Whether you are interested in growing vegetables, herbs, or flowers, container gardening offers a world of opportunities for creativity and exploration.

So, embrace the joys of container gardening and start growing your own garden today! Happy gardening!

BOOK 4:

Seasonal Gardening

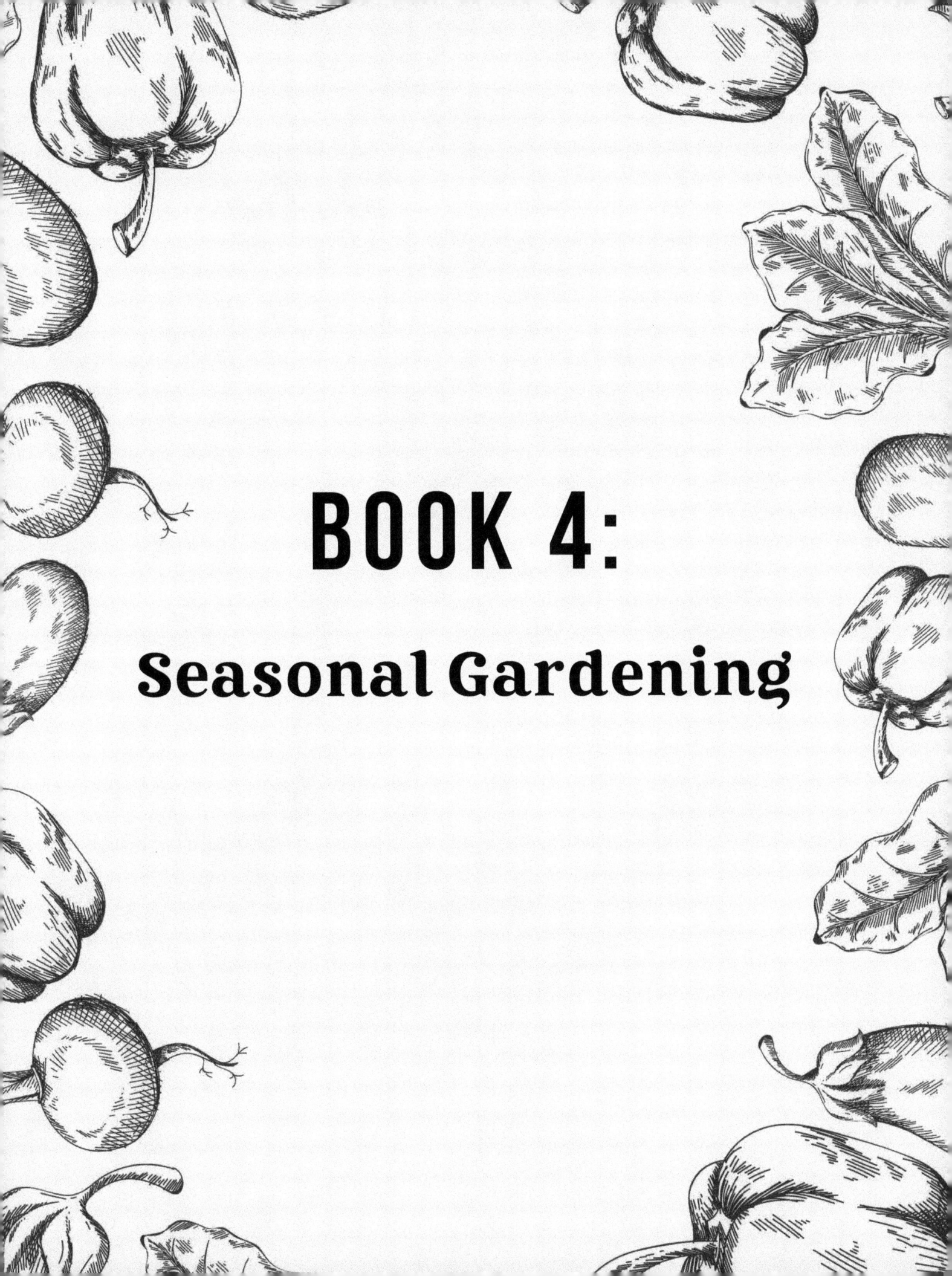

FARM FR

Introduction

Welcome to the wonderful world of seasonal gardening! Gardening is a joyful and rewarding hobby, but it can also be challenging, especially when it comes to knowing when and what to plant. This is where seasonal gardening comes in. By growing plants in harmony with the changing seasons, you can create a beautiful and bountiful garden that provides you with fresh flowers and vegetables throughout the year.

In this book, we will explore the benefits of seasonal gardening and show you how to create a thriving garden that adapts to the changing seasons. You will learn about the best plants for each season, how to prepare your soil, and the techniques for planting, growing, and harvesting your crops. Whether you have a small balcony or a large yard, you will find everything you need to know to create a garden that is tailored to your specific needs and the natural rhythms of the seasons.

Understanding the Growing Seasons in Your Area

One of the most important aspects of seasonal gardening is understanding the growing seasons in your area. This knowledge will help you determine when to plant your crops and which plants are best suited to your climate.

Growing Season Map

A growing season map is a visual representation of the length of time between the last frost date in spring and the first frost date in fall. This map is a useful tool for determining the length of your growing season and the best time to plant crops in your area. Most growing season maps are based on data collected over many years and provide an average length of the growing season.

Zone Map

A zone map is another useful tool for determining the best plants for your area. This map is based on average low temperatures and is divided into hardiness zones, with each zone representing a specific range of temperatures. For example, Zone 7 has an average low temperature of 0°F to 10°F, while Zone 10 has an average low temperature of 30°F to 40°F. By using a zone map, you can determine which plants are best suited to your area based on their ability to tolerate the average low temperatures in your area.

How to Use Them Together

By combining the information from both the growing season map and the zone map, you can make informed decisions about what to plant and when. For example, if you live in an area with a short growing season, you may want to choose crops that mature quickly, such as lettuce, radishes, and spinach. If you live in a warm climate, you may want to choose heat-loving crops such as tomatoes, peppers, and cucumbers.

It is important to remember that both the growing season map and the zone map are based on average data and may not reflect the specific conditions in your area. To get a more accurate picture of the growing seasons in your area, you may want to talk to local gardeners, check local weather records, or consult with your local extension service.

In conclusion, by using the growing season map and the zone map, you can gain a better understanding of the growing seasons in your area and make informed decisions about what to plant and when. With this information in hand, you can create a thriving seasonal garden that is tailored to your specific needs and the natural rhythms of the seasons.

Choosing the Right Crops for Each Season

One of the key elements of seasonal gardening is choosing the right crops for each season. By selecting crops that are well-suited to the current weather conditions, you can create a garden that is not only beautiful but also provides you with fresh, healthy food throughout the year.

Spring Crops

Spring is the perfect time to plant cool-season crops, such as lettuce, spinach, peas, and radishes. These crops are able to tolerate cool temperatures and can be planted as soon as the soil can be worked in the spring. In addition, many spring crops are fast-maturing, making them ideal for gardeners with short growing seasons.

Summer Crops

During the summer, the focus should be on warm-season crops, such as tomatoes, peppers, eggplant, and cucumbers. These crops require warm temperatures and plenty of sunlight to thrive. When planting summer crops, it is important to wait until the soil and air have warmed up to avoid stunting the growth of the plants.

Fall Crops

Fall is the ideal time to plant cool-season crops, such as kale, broccoli, cauliflower, and Brussels sprouts. These crops are able to tolerate cool temperatures and can be planted in late summer or early fall. Fall crops typically mature more slowly than spring crops, so it is important to plan accordingly.

Winter Crops

While many gardeners assume that gardening is not possible during the winter, there are actually several crops that can be grown during the colder months. These crops, such as carrots, beets, and turnips, are able to tolerate cold temperatures and can be planted in late fall for a winter harvest.

When choosing crops for each season, it is important to consider the specific growing conditions in your area, including the length of the growing season, the average temperature, and the amount of sunlight. By selecting crops that are well-suited to the current weather conditions, you can create a garden that provides you with fresh, healthy food throughout the year.

Succession Planting

Succession planting is a gardening technique that involves planting crops in stages in order to maximize the growing season and increase the overall yield. This technique involves planting a new crop in the same space as soon as the previous crop has been harvested, effectively making use of the same space throughout the growing season.

Techniques

There are several techniques that can be used when succession planting, including intercropping, relay planting, and crop rotation. Intercropping involves planting two or more crops in the same space at the same time. For example, planting lettuce and radishes in the same bed. Relay planting involves planting a new crop before the previous crop has been harvested, so that the new crop can mature while the previous crop is still producing. Crop rotation involves planting different crops in the same space each year in order to reduce the build-up of pests and diseases.

Timing

The timing of succession planting is crucial in order to maximize the growing season and increase the overall yield. Generally, the first crop should be planted as soon as the soil can be worked in the spring, with successive crops being planted at regular intervals throughout the growing season. The exact timing will depend on the specific crops being grown and the growing conditions in your area, but it is important to plan ahead in order to ensure that the garden is producing crops continuously throughout the growing season.

In order to determine the best timing for succession planting, it is important to consider the length of the growing season, the average temperature, and the amount of sunlight in your area. For example, in areas with a long growing season, it may be possible to plant crops in the spring, summer, and fall, while in areas with a shorter growing season, it may be necessary to focus on spring and fall planting only.

To conclude, succession planting is a gardening technique that involves planting crops in stages in order to maximize the growing season and increase the overall yield. By using this technique, gardeners can ensure that their garden is producing crops continuously throughout the growing season, providing them with fresh, healthy food from their own garden. With proper planning and timing, anyone can create a thriving garden using the technique of succession planting.

How to Preserve Your Harvest

Gardening can be a rewarding and fulfilling experience, but what do you do with all that produce once it's ready to be harvested? Preserving your harvest is a great way to ensure that you can enjoy the fruits of your labor throughout the year, even when fresh produce is out of season. There are several methods for preserving your harvest, including canning, freezing, drying, and fermenting.

Canning

Canning is a method of preserving food by sealing it in airtight jars and heating it to a high temperature to kill bacteria and other microorganisms. This method is ideal for high-acid foods, such as fruits, pickles, and most tomatoes, as the acid in these foods helps to prevent the growth of harmful bacteria.

To start canning, you'll need to gather jars, lids, and rings, as well as a canner or large pot with a lid. Fill the jars with the prepared food, leaving some headspace, and then place the lids and rings on the jars. Place the jars in the canner, making sure that they are covered with water, and then bring the water to a boil. Process the jars for the recommended time, and then remove them from the canner and allow them to cool completely.

Freezing

Freezing is a simple and convenient way to preserve your harvest, as it requires no special equipment or preparation. Simply wash, chop, and freeze your produce in airtight containers or freezer bags, and then thaw and use as needed. This method is best for fruits and vegetables that are not typically canned, such as berries, leafy greens, and beans.

Drying

Drying is a traditional method of preserving food that has been used for centuries. This method involves removing the moisture from food, either by air-drying or using a dehydrator, in order to prevent the growth of bacteria and other microorganisms. Dried foods can be stored for several months and can be rehydrated for use in recipes.

Fermenting

Fermenting is a method of preserving food that involves allowing bacteria to break down the carbohydrates in the food, creating lactic acid and preserving the food in the process. Fermented foods are not only a great way to preserve your harvest, but they are also rich in probiotics, which can improve gut health.

In conclusion, preserving your harvest is a great way to ensure that you can enjoy the fruits of your labor throughout the year. Whether you choose to can, freeze, dry, or ferment your produce, you'll be able to enjoy fresh, healthy food even when fresh produce is out of season. With a little preparation and the right techniques, anyone can preserve their harvest and enjoy fresh, healthy food all year long.

Tips For Maximizing Your Reserves

Use napkins for lettuce - Not only lettuce, but chicory, radicchio, valerian and other leafy greens last much longer when associated with napkins or tea towels. You can use this technique with both bagged and head salads. Simply insert a paper towel inside the package once it has been opened, or wrap washed and dried salad leaves around a dishcloth. The paper and cloth will absorb moisture, stop the leaves from deteriorating, and allow you to extend your salad for 5 more days.

Store aromatic herbs in a jar of water - *did you know that?* You harvest herbs and immediately see them wilting, darkening, and losing vigor. A solution? Soak the harvested herbs inside a jar with fresh water, which you will empty as soon as you need to use them. Be careful, though! This technique prolongs their freshness for only 2 more days.

Vegetables and bananas don't get along - You may already know that bananas absolutely do not go in the refrigerator, but did you also know that bananas should stay away from many vegetables? In fact, bananas release ethylene, a gas that speeds up the ripening process, causing vegetables to deteriorate much faster.

Put tomatoes upside down - To store tomatoes out of the refrigerator place them on a tray or baking sheet, and position them with the stem pointing downward. This position eliminates air infiltration and thus their ripening.

Store carrots underwater - Just as with herbs, carrots stay fresher inside a jar filled, and sealed, with fresh water. Clean the carrots and place them vertically inside a jar that can hold them entirely. Fill the jar with water and place it in the refrigerator. Every 2 to 3 days change the water because it may turn orange because of the carotene; eat them all within a week!

Preparing for the Next Season

After a successful growing season, it's important to prepare your garden for the next season. This involves a combination of fall cleanup, soil amendment, and other tasks that will help ensure that your garden is ready to thrive when spring arrives.

Fall Cleanup

Fall cleanup is an essential step in preparing your garden for the next season. This involves removing dead or diseased plant material, as well as cleaning up fallen leaves and other debris. By removing this material, you'll help prevent the spread of diseases and pests, and make it easier to work in your garden in the spring.

Soil Amendment

Soil amendment is the process of improving the quality of your soil, either by adding organic matter or by adjusting the pH. Soil amendment is especially important in areas where the soil is poor, as this can impact the health and growth of your plants. Adding compost, leaves, or other organic matter to your soil can help improve soil structure, increase nutrient availability, and improve water retention.

In addition to soil amendment, it's also important to consider other tasks that can help prepare your garden for the next season. This may include mulching, covering crops with row covers, and planting cover crops to help improve soil health and reduce erosion.

In conclusion, preparing your garden for the next season is an essential step in ensuring a successful growing season. Whether you're focusing on fall cleanup, soil amendment, or other tasks, taking the time to properly prepare your garden now will help ensure that it's ready to thrive when spring arrives. With a little preparation and attention to detail, you can create a healthy and productive garden that will provide you with fresh, healthy produce year after year.

Conclusion

Gardening is a true labor of love, a hobby that provides a connection to nature and the satisfaction of growing your own food. Seasonal gardening takes this to a new level, as it allows you to work with the natural cycles of the seasons to grow crops that are perfectly suited to your climate and conditions. This book has served as a comprehensive guide to seasonal gardening, including the details on understanding growing seasons, choosing the right crops for each season, the benefits of succession planting, preserving your harvest, and preparing for the next season. By following the information and techniques provided, you'll be able to create a thriving garden that will produce an abundant harvest year after year.

BOOK 5:

Gardening Hacks

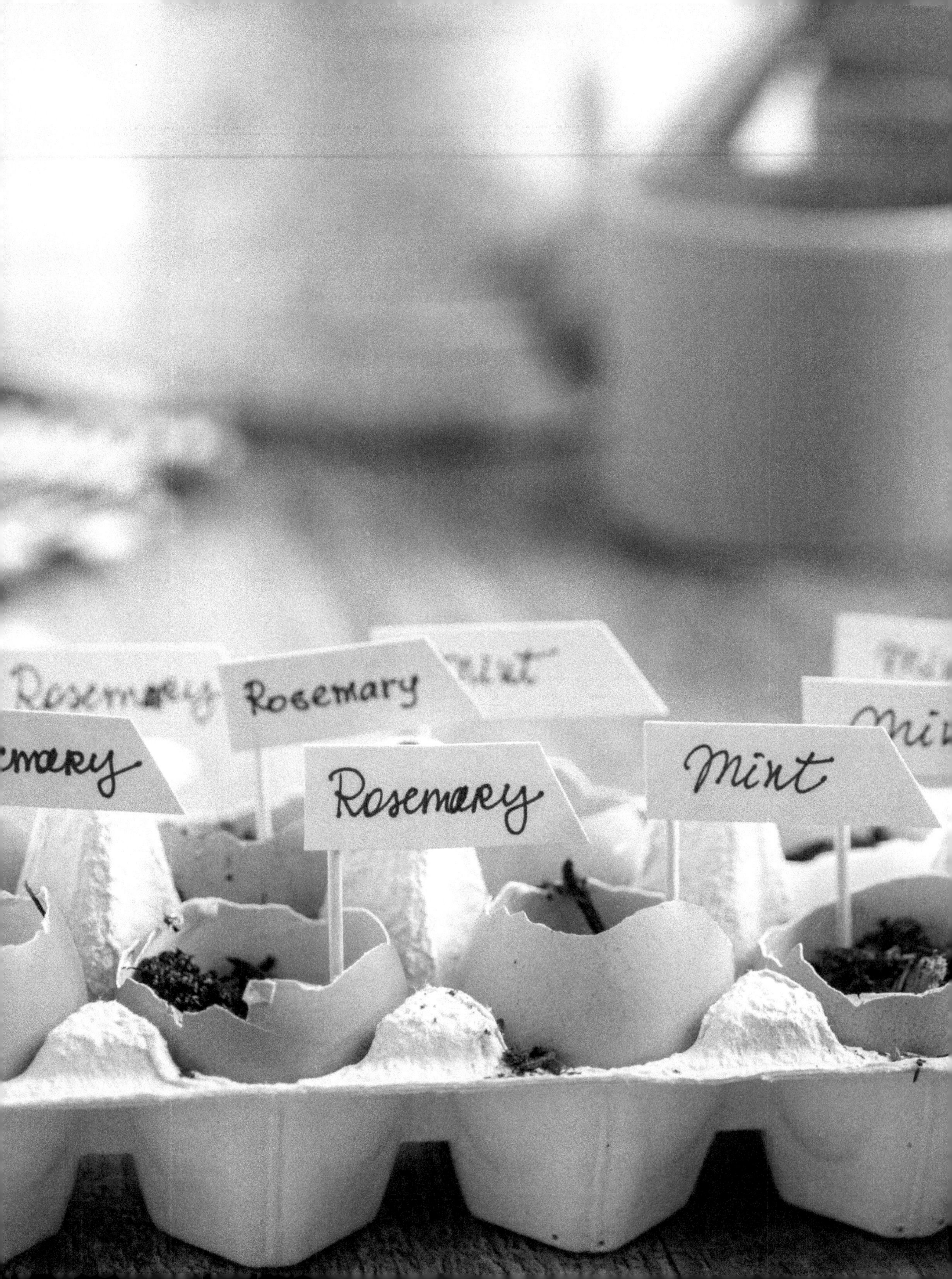
Rosemary
Rosemary
Rosemary
Mint

Introduction

Gardening is a wonderful hobby that provides endless benefits - from growing your own fresh produce to creating a peaceful outdoor space. But, let's be honest, it can also be a bit overwhelming at times. There's so much to learn about soil preparation, plant selection, pest management, and more. That's why we've created this book, to share with you some of the most innovative and effective gardening hacks that will make your gardening experience more manageable, efficient, and fun.

Whether you're a seasoned gardener or just starting out, this book is packed with tips and tricks that will help you get the most out of your garden. From using coffee grounds to deter pests, to making your own compost, to creating the perfect garden bed in a raised container, we've got you covered. These hacks are easy to implement, and they'll save you time, money, and effort while maximizing your garden's potential.

Maximizing Small Spaces & Productivity

Gardening is a great hobby, but it can be challenging when you have limited space to work with. Fortunately, there are many strategies you can use to maximize small spaces and increase productivity. In this chapter, we'll explore some of the most effective techniques for making the most of your garden space, including:

- **Vertical Gardening:** This technique involves growing plants upward, either on a wall, trellis, or other vertical structure. This can be a great way to add more growing space in a small area, and it also makes it easier to care for your plants and harvest your crops.

- **Intercropping:** Intercropping is the practice of planting two or more crops in close proximity to each other. This technique can be used to maximize space, increase productivity, and even help control pests and diseases.

- **Pruning**: Regular pruning is an important part of maximizing small spaces and increasing productivity. Pruning helps maintain plant health and growth, and it can also be used to control the size and shape of your plants.

- **Mulching:** Mulching is the practice of covering the soil around your plants with organic material, such as leaves, straw, or wood chips. Mulching helps to conserve moisture, suppress weeds, and regulate soil temperature, all of which can improve the health and productivity of your plants.

- **Maximizing Light:** Light is an essential factor for plant growth, and maximizing the amount of light that reaches your plants can help increase productivity. You can use mirrors or aluminum foil to reflect more light onto your plants, or place them in areas where they will receive maximum sunlight.

By using these techniques, you'll be able to make the most of your small garden space and increase your garden's productivity.

Money-Saving Tips

While vegetable gardening provides many benefits, it can also come with a cost. From buying pots, soil, and seeds to providing adequate water, light, and nutrition, the expenses can add up quickly. However, there are many simple and practical ways to save money while still maintaining a healthy and thriving vegetable garden. In this chapter, we will explore different tips and tricks to protect your savings while enhancing the sustainability of your garden.

REGROWING VEGGIES FROM KITCHEN SCRAPS

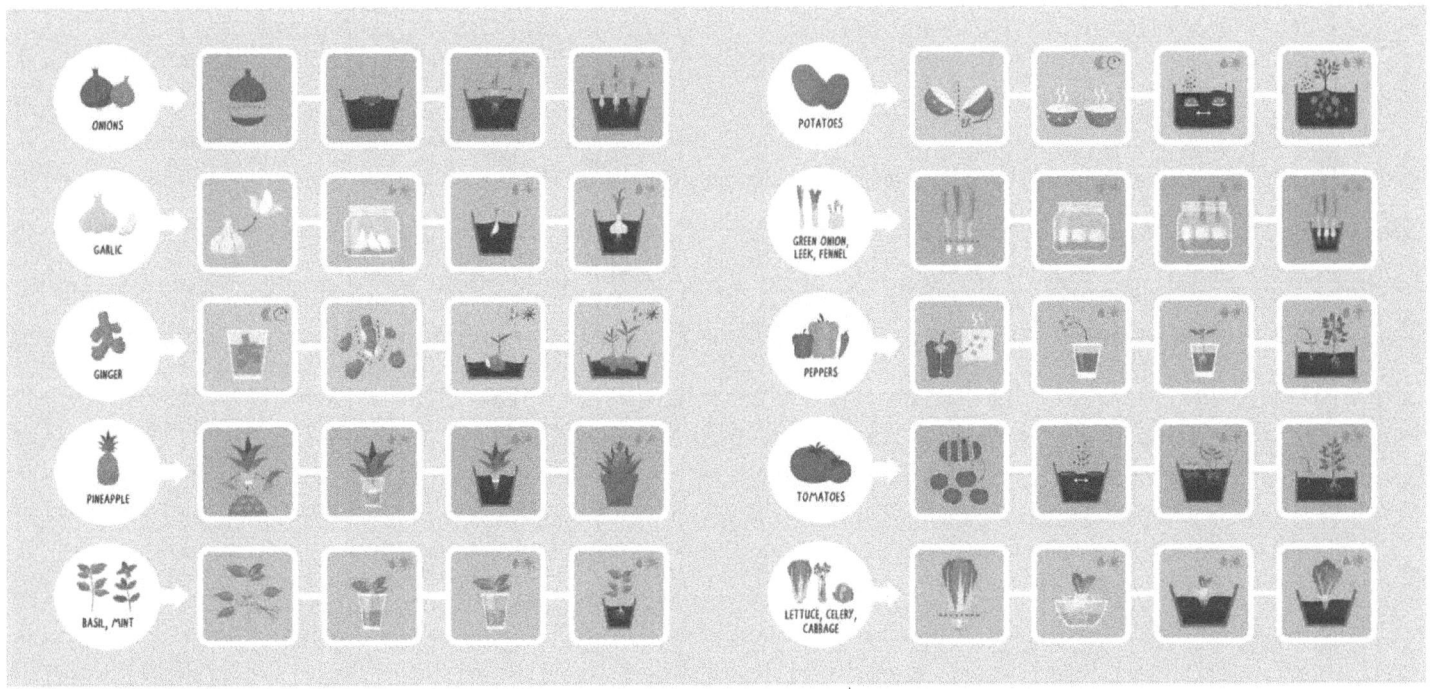

Did you know you can regrow many of your favorite vegetables right from your kitchen scraps? With just a little bit of effort and a few simple materials, you can enjoy fresh, homegrown produce all year round.

Regrowing vegetables from kitchen scraps is a great way to reduce food waste, save money, and provide yourself with a continuous supply of fresh produce. Many popular vegetables can be regrown in this way, including lettuce, celery, green onions, garlic, lemongrass, ginger, and even potatoes.

Before you begin, make sure you have the following materials:

- Clean containers with drainage holes
- Potting soil

- Water

Instructions:

Step 1: Choose your vegetable scraps. Look for scraps with healthy, plump roots or a sprout. You may need to let the scraps sit out overnight so they can dry out a bit.

Step 2: Fill your containers with potting soil and plant your vegetable scraps. Be sure to plant them deep enough so that the roots or sprouts are covered by soil.

Step 3: Water your regrowing vegetables regularly, but make sure not to over-water them. Most vegetables need to be kept moist but not waterlogged.

Step 4: Place your containers in a sunny spot and wait for your vegetables to grow. Depending on the vegetable, it may take anywhere from a few days to a few weeks to see new growth.

Now that you have successfully regrown your vegetables, you can continue to care for them by following the guidelines for each vegetable. As they grow, you can harvest them and enjoy fresh, homegrown produce right from your kitchen scraps. It's important to remember that regrowing vegetables from kitchen scraps is a low-cost, low-maintenance activity that requires very little space. So, whether you're a seasoned gardener or just starting out, give regrowing vegetables a try and see the satisfaction of providing your family with fresh, homegrown food.

Top 10 Money Saving Crops

Growing your own food can be a fun, rewarding, and cost-effective way to save money on groceries. But not all crops are equal when it comes to cost savings. Here are 10 of the most budget-friendly crops to consider for your container garden.

- **Leafy greens:** Lettuce, spinach, and other leafy greens are fast-growing and provide a lot of food for a relatively small investment in seeds or seedlings. They're also versatile and can be used in salads, sandwiches, and stir-fries.

- **Herbs:** Growing your own herbs can save you money on expensive dried or fresh herbs from the store. Plus, you can always have fresh herbs on hand for cooking. Consider growing basil, cilantro, parsley, and mint.

- **Radishes:** Radishes are easy to grow and mature quickly, making them a great choice for container gardeners. They're also a tasty and nutritious addition to salads and sandwiches.

- **Green beans:** Green beans are another fast-growing crop that can provide a lot of food in a short amount of time. They're also a staple in many meals and can be eaten raw or cooked.

- **Peppers:** Bell peppers and hot peppers can be expensive at the grocery store, but they're easy to grow in containers and will produce a bountiful harvest. They're also versatile and can be used in a variety of dishes.

- **Tomatoes:** Tomatoes are a staple in many meals and can be used in a variety of dishes, from sauces to salads. They're also relatively easy to grow in containers and will provide a lot of food for the effort.

- **Carrots:** Carrots are nutritious and tasty root vegetables that can be grown in containers. They may take a bit longer to mature than some other crops, but they're worth the wait.

- **Squash:** Summer and winter squashes are a great option for container gardeners. They're relatively easy to grow and will provide a lot of food for the effort. They're also versatile and can be used in a variety of dishes.

- **Garlic:** Garlic is a staple in many kitchens and is relatively easy to grow in containers. Just plant a single clove and watch it grow into a full bulb. You can also plant several cloves for a larger harvest.

- **Peas:** Peas are a fast-growing and nutritious crop that can be grown in containers. They're also versatile and can be used in salads, stir-fries, and as a side dish.

Plant Propagation

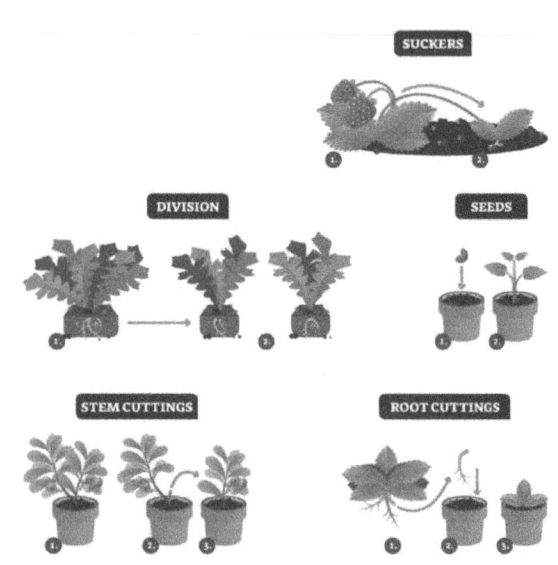

Plant propagation is the process of producing new plants from existing ones. In container gardening, propagation is an efficient way to increase your collection of plants without having to buy new seeds or seedlings. The method of propagation will depend on the type of plant you are working with, but some common methods include cuttings, division, and layering.

Cuttings

Cuttings are the simplest and most common method of propagation in container gardening. Cuttings are taken from the parent plant and then rooted in water or soil to grow new plants. The cutting should be a healthy, non-flowering stem that is 3-6 inches long. The bottom of the stem should be cut just below a node and the top of the stem should have a few leaves. Cuttings can be placed in water or directly into the soil, but it is important to provide adequate moisture and light to promote rooting.

Step-by-Step Process:

1. Choose healthy and mature plants to take cuttings.
2. Cut a 4-6 inch stem from the parent plant with a sharp, clean knife or scissors.
3. Remove any leaves from the bottom 2 inches of the stem and dip the cut end into rooting hormone powder.
4. Fill a small pot with well-draining potting mix and make a hole in the center.
5. Insert the cutting into the hole and gently press the soil around it to secure it in place.
6. Water the cutting until the soil is moist but not soggy.
7. Cover the pot with plastic wrap to create a greenhouse effect and place it in a warm, bright location out of direct sunlight.
8. Check the soil regularly and water it as needed to keep it moist.
9. After 4-6 weeks, the cutting should have formed roots and can be planted in a larger pot or garden bed.

Division

Division is a method of propagation that involves separating the parent plant into multiple parts, each with roots and shoots, to create new plants. Division is best for perennials and bulbs, such as daffodils, lilies, and daylilies. To divide a plant, gently remove it from the pot and separate it into smaller pieces, ensuring each piece has an adequate amount of roots and shoots. Re-pot each section into its own container and water thoroughly.

Step-by-Step Process:

1. Choose a mature plant that is in need of division.
2. Water the plant thoroughly the day before dividing it.
3. Dig the plant up from the garden or carefully remove it from the pot.
4. Use a sharp, clean knife or shovel to divide the root ball into smaller sections.
5. Replant each section in its own pot filled with fresh potting mix or in a garden bed.
6. Water the newly divided plants thoroughly and place them in a warm, bright location.
7. Monitor the soil moisture levels and water as needed to keep it consistently moist.
8. Fertilize the newly divided plants to encourage growth and promote healthy root development.

Layering

Layering is a method of propagation that involves rooting a stem while it is still attached to the parent plant. To layer a plant, choose a low-growing stem and bend it towards the ground, burying the bottom part of the stem in the soil. Once the stem has rooted, it can be detached from the parent plant and re-potted into its own container.

Step-by-Step Process:

1. Choose a healthy and mature parent plant.
2. Locate a stem that is near the ground and bend it gently to the soil level.
3. Use a sharp, clean knife to make a shallow cut in the stem about 1 inch long.
4. Apply rooting hormone powder to the cut and bury the stem in the soil.
5. Secure the buried stem in place with a small rock or peg.

6. Water the area regularly and keep the soil moist but not soggy.

7. After several weeks, roots should have formed along the buried stem.

8. Cut the newly rooted stem from the parent plant and plant it in its own pot filled with fresh potting mix or in a garden bed.

9. Water the newly rooted plant thoroughly and place it in a warm, bright location.

10. Monitor the soil moisture levels and water as needed to keep it consistently moist.

Growing & Harvesting Tips

Growing and harvesting tips are key to maximizing the productivity of your garden and ensuring that you get the most from your crops. Here are some tips for fast harvests, growing berries in containers, perennials, and growing vegetables in a bottle:

FAST-GROWING VEGETABLES

If you are looking to have fresh produce from your garden quickly, then this chapter is for you. Here, we will be discussing ten of the fastest-growing vegetables and herbs that you can harvest in no time. Whether you have limited space or simply want to enjoy the fruits (and vegetables) of your labor sooner, these plants are ideal for quick harvests.

- **Lettuce:** Lettuce is a staple ingredient in many salads and is one of the quickest growing crops. It can be harvested just 30 days after planting and can be grown in containers or in the ground.
- **Arugula:** Arugula is a spicy, flavorful green that can be harvested in just 40 days. It grows best in cool weather and is a great option for spring and fall gardens.
- **Radishes**: Radishes are fast-growing root vegetables that can be harvested in just 25 to 30 days. They are great for adding crunch and flavor to salads and sandwiches.
- **Spinach**: Spinach is a nutritious green that is packed with vitamins and minerals. It grows quickly and can be harvested in just 40 days.
- **Carrots:** Carrots are a sweet, crunchy root vegetable that can be harvested in just 60 to 70 days. They grow best in loose, well-drained soil and can be grown in containers or on the ground.
- **Scallions**: Scallions are a type of green onion that is fast-growing and can be harvested in just 60 days. They are a great addition to soups, stews, and stir-fries.
- **Pea shoots**: Pea shoots are the tendrils of pea plants and are a delicious and nutritious green that can be harvested in just 30 days.
- **Basil:** Basil is a fragrant herb that is commonly used in Mediterranean and Thai cuisine. It grows quickly and can be harvested in just 60 days.
- **Cilantro:** Cilantro is a fresh, flavorful herb that is commonly used in Mexican and Asian cuisine. It grows quickly and can be harvested in just 40 days.
- **Swiss Chard:** Swiss Chard is a nutritious leafy green that can be harvested in just 45 days. It grows best in cool weather and is a great option for spring and fall gardens.

Growing Berries In Containers

Growing delicious berries in containers can be a rewarding and easy way to have fresh fruit on hand. Whether you have a small balcony or a large patio, container gardening can provide a great opportunity to cultivate your own fresh berries. Here is some guidance to help you grow delicious berries in containers.

- Choose the right containers: When choosing containers for your berry plants, look for ones that are large enough to accommodate the plant's roots, but not so large that the soil will become waterlogged. The container should also have drainage holes to allow excess water to escape. You can use plastic, terra cotta, or wooden containers, but make sure they are sturdy enough to support the plant.

- Choose the right soil: Good quality potting soil that is well-draining is essential for growing berries in containers. You can purchase commercial potting soil or make your own by mixing equal parts of peat moss, compost, and perlite or vermiculite.

- Choose the right location: Berries need full sun to produce the best fruit, so choose a location that gets at least 6 hours of direct sunlight per day. If you live in a hot climate, it's important to provide some shade during the hottest part of the day to prevent the soil from drying out too quickly.

- Watering: Proper watering is essential for growing healthy berries in containers. The soil should be kept consistently moist, but not waterlogged. Water the plants deeply, making sure to soak the root zone, and then allow the soil to drain before watering again. In hot weather, you may need to water your plants daily.

- Fertilizing: Berry plants need regular fertilizing to produce healthy growth and good fruit production. Use a balanced, water-soluble fertilizer, such as a 10-10-10, every 2-3 weeks during the growing season.

- Pruning: Regular pruning is important for maintaining healthy growth and good fruit production. Prune your berry plants in the late winter or early spring, removing any dead, diseased, or crossing branches. This will encourage new growth and help keep the plant compact and productive.

- Pests and Diseases: Berries can be susceptible to pests, such as aphids and spider mites, and diseases, such as powdery mildew. Regular inspections of your plants and prompt treatment of any problems will help keep your berry plants healthy and productive.

How to Grow Blueberries

Blueberries are particularly well suited to container growing, as they are relatively small shrubs that can be pruned to control their size. Below is a step-by-step guide on how to grow delicious blueberries in containers.

Step 1: Selecting the Right Container and Soil

The first step in growing blueberries in containers is to choose the right size and type of container. Blueberries are small shrubs that can reach a height of up to 6 feet and a width of 4 feet, so a container with a depth of at least 18 inches and a diameter of at least 24 inches is recommended. The container should also have at least one drainage hole to prevent water from standing in the bottom and causing root rot.

The soil you use to grow blueberries is just as important as the container. Blueberries prefer a slightly acidic soil with a pH between 4.5 and 5.5. You can buy special blueberry soil from a garden center, or you can create your own mixture by combining equal parts of peat moss, coarse sand, and sphagnum moss.

Step 2: Selecting the Right Blueberry Plant

There are wide different varieties of blueberries, but not all of them are suitable for container growing. The most important factor to consider when selecting a blueberry plant for your container garden is its size. Smaller, dwarf varieties such as "Northblue" or "Top Hat" are ideal, as they can be easily pruned to control their size and will not outgrow your container.

Step 3: Planting the Blueberry Bush

Once you have the right container and soil, it's time to plant your blueberry bush. Fill the bottom of the container with a layer of gravel to improve drainage, then add a layer of soil. Place the blueberry plant in the center of the container, making sure that the top of the root ball is level with the soil surface. Fill in around the plant with more soil, tamping it down gently to remove any air pockets.

Step 4: Watering and Fertilizing the Blueberry Bush

Water your blueberry bush thoroughly after planting, and make sure to keep the soil consistently moist but not waterlogged. During the growing season, blueberries will benefit from regular applications of fertilizer. Use a fertilizer that is specifically formulated for blueberries and follow the instructions on the label for the correct amount and frequency of application.

Step 5: Pruning the Blueberry Bush

Pruning is an important part of growing blueberries in containers, as it helps control the size of the bush and encourages new growth. Prune your blueberry bush in late winter or early spring, cutting back any straggly or crossing branches to maintain a compact shape.

Step 6: Protecting the Blueberry Bush from Pests and Diseases

Blueberries are relatively pest-free and disease-resistant, but it is still important to keep an eye out for any signs of trouble. Common pests that can attack blueberries include aphids, mites, and fruit flies. Diseases such as powdery mildew and botrytis can also be a problem. Keep your blueberry bush healthy by providing adequate water and nutrients, and remove any infected leaves promptly.

THE 4 BEST PERENNIAL VEGETABLES

Perennial vegetables are a great way to reduce the amount of work required in the garden. These vegetables come back year after year, eliminating the need to replant and reducing the amount of work required to maintain your garden. Here are four of the best perennial vegetables that you can add to your garden:

1. **Globe Artichoke:** The Globe Artichoke is a beautiful, architectural plant that produces large, edible flower heads and can reach up to 5 feet tall. These hearty plants love full sun and well-draining soil with a pH between 6.0 and 7.0. Although they can handle dry conditions, watering regularly will result in better yields. Fertilizing monthly during the growing season with a balanced fertilizer will also keep your Globe Artichokes thriving. *Oh, and did I mention they can withstand temperatures as low as 20°F?*

2. **Babington's Leeks:** These cold-tolerant perennials are perfect for gardeners in colder climates. They prefer full sun and well-draining soil with a pH between 6.0 and 7.0, and regular watering will lead to better yields. A monthly dose of balanced fertilizer during the growing season will keep your Babington's Leeks healthy and happy.

3. **Perennial Kale**: These hardy greens thrive in full sun and well-draining soil with a pH between 6.0 and 7.0. While they can handle dry conditions, regular watering will result in the best yields. Like Babington's Leeks, Perennial Kales are also well-suited for colder climates and can handle low temperatures. A monthly dose of balanced fertilizer during the growing season will keep your Perennial Kale plants thriving.

4. **Asparagus:** This delicious and nutritious perennial loves full sun and well-draining soil with a pH between 6.5 and 7.5. Regular watering will lead to better yields, and a monthly dose of balanced fertilizer during the growing season will keep your Asparagus plants healthy and happy. And, like Globe Artichokes, Asparagus can also handle temperatures as low as 20°F.

These four perennials offer a tasty and low-maintenance option for your vegetable garden. By providing the right growing conditions, including full sun, well-draining soil, regular watering, and balanced fertilization, you can look forward to years of delicious and nutritious harvests.

Growing Vegetables In A Bottle

Growing vegetables in a bottle is a great way to maximize small spaces. This method involves planting seeds in a bottle filled with water and growing medium. The roots grow in the water and the tops of the plants grow out of the bottle. With this technique, you may grow food in confined areas like flats or balconies, control the soil and water levels, and limit the risk of pests and diseases. Before you begin, there are a few other things to think about.

Essential Things to Think About

- **The type of vegetable:** Pick veggies that thrive in containers, such as cherry tomatoes, lettuce, spinach, herbs, and radishes. Avoid growing larger veggies because they require a larger container, such as corn or pumpkins.

- **The size of the bottle:** Take into account the bottle's dimensions and ensure it is big enough to accommodate the vegetable's root system. Most small to medium-sized plants will fit well in a two-liter bottle.

- **Drainage:** Your plants' health depends on proper drainage. To allow extra water to drain, ensure the bottle's bottom has several holes.

- **Light:** The majority of vegetables require at least six hours per day of direct sunshine. Artificial lights can be used to give your plants the essential light if a sunny location is not available.

Step-by-Step Process

1. **Prepare the Bottle:** Clean and dry a plastic bottle. Turn the bottle upside down after cutting off the top third of it. Create several tiny drainage holes in the bottom of the bottle using a sharp knife or pair of scissors.

2. **Fill the Bottom of the Bottle with Soil:** Make sure the soil in the bottom of the bottle is tightly packed and of high quality.

3. **Plant the Seeds:** Place your seeds in the soil and cover them with a thin layer. Be sure to adhere to the seed packet's planting depth and spacing recommendations.

4. **Water the Seeds:** Water the soil gently, being careful not to disturb the seeds. Put the bottle's lid on, then set it somewhere sunny.

5. **Maintain the Plants:** Regularly water the soil, carefully keeping it moist but not soggy. To ensure your plants get all the required nutrients, fertilize them every two weeks.

6. **Harvest Your Vegetables:** You can harvest your plants once they've developed fruit and are ready to be enjoyed.

Growing your own food is easy and sustainable in plastic bottle gardens. You can have fresh vegetables at your fingertips with simple tools and perseverance. To begin your journey of producing vegetables, remember the crucial things to take into account and follow the step-by-step instructions.

Conclusion

The world of gardening is full of surprises and there is always something new to discover. Gardening hacks can make this journey even more exciting and can help you to maximize your garden's potential. Whether you are a seasoned gardener or a beginner, these hacks can help you to achieve your gardening goals and create a beautiful, bountiful garden that will bring joy to your life.

The beauty of gardening is that it is a never-ending journey, always filled with new challenges and opportunities to learn and grow. With the right tools and techniques, you can turn any space into a thriving garden that provides fresh produce, stunning flowers, and a peaceful environment. So take what you have learned in this book, step outside, and get your hands dirty. Happy gardening!

BONUS: Electroculture

Introduction

It has been shown that "electroculture," the use of electric and electromagnetic fields in farming and gardening, improves plant growth, nutrient uptake, and resistance to diseases and pests. Recent years have seen a rise in the use of this technique as a result of the increasing global demand for food and the importance of using environmentally friendly agricultural methods.

Electroculture in vegetable gardening stands out as a significant alternative or supplementary methods to conventional methods like the application of chemical fertilizers and pesticides. Electrical stimulation can be used by gardeners to increase crop yields, reduce the use of chemical inputs, and promote healthier, disease- and pest-resistant plants. By lessening the toll that gardening takes on the planet and maximizing efficiency in the use of available resources, electroculture contributes to the overarching objective of sustainable agriculture.

The purpose of this chapter is to provide a foundational understanding of electroculture, an overview of the various methods that make up this approach, and a discussion of the equipment needed to put these principles into practice in a home vegetable garden. The potential of this innovative approach to sustainable agriculture is explored, along with the benefits and drawbacks of using electroculture techniques in vegetable gardening.

Basic Principles of Electroculture

An essential tenet of electroculture is that plants' growth and development are profoundly influenced by the presence of electric and electromagnetic fields. Several physiological processes in plants may be influenced by these fields; these include nutrient uptake, water absorption, cell division, and photosynthesis. Their impact on plant signaling and communication pathways may also lead to increased resistance to diseases and pests.

There are several primary methods for applying electrical stimulation to vegetable plants, each with its own quirks and growth effects. One method involves using a steady electrical field applied to the plants, which is called direct current (DC). To do this, electrodes are buried and connected to a DC power supply. Direct current has the potential to alter the movement of ions in the soil, which in turn may alter the uptake of nutrients by the plant's roots.

Electrical stimulation with alternating current (AC) involves periodically reversing the direction of the applied electric field. AC electromagnetic fields can permeate plant tissues, potentially altering plant cellular and systemic processes. Controlling the electrical conductivity of the soil is just one component of electroculture, which also makes use of electricity to promote plant growth.

Pulsed electromagnetic fields (PEMF) are also used for electrical stimulation in electroculture. Short bursts of electromagnetic energy at specific frequencies and intensities are used in pulsed electromagnetic field therapy (PEMF) on plants. Plant cells and tissues may respond to these pulses by altering signaling pathways, gene expression, and metabolic processes. Plants benefit from pulsed electromagnetic fields (PEMF) in a number of ways, including enhanced germination, enhanced nutrient uptake, and enhanced resistance to stress and disease.

Electroculture Techniques for Vegetable Gardening

This section describes a variety of techniques for controlling soil electrical conductivity, including plasma farming, electrostatic field applications, and more. Each strategy is broken down, and concrete examples of how to implement them in a backyard vegetable garden are provided.

Electrostatic Field Application

The first step in getting your garden up and running is choosing a voltage generator. You'll need it to generate sufficient voltage for whichever method you choose for applying an electrostatic field. Find out what voltage levels work best for the plants you plan to grow vegetables.

- **Set up the electrodes:** The electrodes will be the metal poles or stakes you will obtain. Distribute them uniformly, then raise them to a height that will keep them well above the plants, and finally, set them up vertically all around your garden bed. Changing the space between the electrodes and the plants modifies the intensity of the electrostatic field.
- **Connect the electrodes to the voltage generator:** Insulated wires should be used to connect the electrodes to the power source. Make sure the wires aren't dangling and causing a hazard before you start using them.
- **Turn on the voltage generator:** Connect the electrodes and activate the voltage generator to create an electrostatic field. If the field is having a negative effect on your plants, try increasing the voltage or moving the electrodes.

Soil Electrical Conductivity Management

The soil's ideal electrical conductivity needs to be established. Determine the electrical conductivity range ideal for growing the vegetables of your choice. This information can be found in horticultural magazines, online, and in discussions with local experts.

- **Measure the current soil electrical conductivity**: Use a soil conductivity meter to measure the electrical conductivity of your garden's soil. This will serve as a baseline for comparison as you implement changes.

- **Adjust soil moisture:** Soil electrical conductivity is influenced by moisture content. To increase conductivity, water your garden more frequently or thoroughly. To decrease conductivity, reduce the amount or frequency of watering.
- **Modify salt content:** Adding or removing salts from the soil can also affect electrical conductivity. To increase conductivity, add soluble salts, such as potassium or calcium chloride. To decrease conductivity, leach salts from the soil by applying a high volume of water and allowing it to drain.
- **Apply electrical currents (optional):** In some cases, applying electrical currents directly to the soil may be helpful in achieving the desired conductivity levels. Connect your voltage generator to buried electrodes in the soil and adjust the voltage accordingly.

Plasma Agriculture

Acquire a plasma generator: Purchase a low-temperature plasma generator suitable for agricultural use or build one using DIY instructions available online. Ensure that the generator meets the safety requirements and specifications for your intended application.

- **Set up the plasma generator:** Position the plasma generator in a safe location near your garden. Attach the necessary electrodes or applicators to the generator and route them to the area where you want to apply the plasma.
- **Apply plasma to the plants:** Turn on the plasma generator and apply the plasma directly to the plants. Depending on your specific goals, you may choose to apply the plasma as a one-time treatment or continuously throughout the growing season. Be sure to follow the recommended guidelines for your specific vegetable plants and plasma generator.
- **Monitor the effects:** Regularly observe the impact of the plasma treatment on your plants, adjusting the application method, duration, or intensity as needed. Keep track of the results to determine the efficacy of plasma agriculture for your vegetable garden.

Seed Treatment with Electromagnetic Fields

When used properly, electromagnetic fields can stimulate plant growth and development in vegetable crops. You should research the optimal parameters of electromagnetic fields (such as frequency, intensity, and duration) before beginning to treat the seeds of your chosen vegetable plants. This information can be obtained from specialized interviews or the scholarly literature.

The next step is to gather the seeds and put them in a non-conductive dish made of glass or plastic. Distribute the seeds so that none of them are touching. You should place an electromagnetic field generator designed for seeds very close to the container containing the seeds. Attach any antennas or implements needed to bring the seeds within the sphere of influence of the electromagnetic field.

Put the seeds in an electromagnetic field with the parameters you found in your research, and turn on the generator. Keep a close eye on the treatment to make sure everything is going as planned. Once the process is complete, the seeds can be planted in your garden as usual. By comparing the germination and growth of treated seeds to those of untreated seeds, we can ascertain the efficacy of the electromagnetic field treatment.

MAGNETIZED WATER IRRIGATION

If you want your vegetable plants to be healthier and grow faster, try irrigating them with magnetized water. The benefits of magnetized water, such as enhanced nutrient uptake, accelerated growth, and resistance to diseases and pests, are among the first things you should look into. The following step is to acquire or make a water magnetizer to use with your garden's sprinkler system. Make sure the magnetizer's flow rate and magnet strength are adequate.

Connect the water magnetizer to your garden's preexisting irrigation system per the manufacturer's instructions or provided guidelines, making sure it is installed securely and does not obstruct water flow. Now that the water has been magnetized, you can use it to water your garden as usual. Be sure to monitor the progress of your plants after introducing the magnetized water.

You can improve plant growth and harvest by experimenting with various electroculture techniques to find the one that works best for your vegetable garden. As with any novel gardening approach, you should monitor results closely and make adjustments as needed to achieve your desired outcomes.

Equipment and Setup for Home Gardeners

Necessary Equipment

Equipment such as electrodes, voltage generators, monitoring devices, and safety gear are necessary for successful application of electroculture techniques in a home garden. The specific tools required for an electroculture project will vary depending on the method chosen.

Electrodes, which are essential for transmitting electricity to plants or soil, can be constructed from sturdy, rust-resistant metal stakes, poles, or wires. Commercially available or homemade voltage generators can be used to produce the necessary voltage for various electroculture applications. In order to achieve the best outcomes, it is crucial to track the effects of electrical stimulation on plants and soil using monitoring devices such as conductivity meters, pH meters, and moisture sensors.

Finally, safety is of the utmost importance when dealing with electricity. Wearing gloves, non-conductive footwear, and safety glasses will protect you from electrical shock and other injuries that could occur while using electroculture techniques in your garden.

Setting Up and Maintaining Equipment

Careful planning before implementing electroculture techniques in your garden can ensure the most efficient placement of electrodes, voltage generators, and monitoring devices. For electroculture to be effective, it is imperative that the electrodes be installed in a safe location, far from any soil or plants.

Next, insulated wires are used to link the voltage source to the electrodes. Care must be taken so that nobody gets a shock or trips over the wires. Checked and functioning conductivity meters, pH meters, and moisture sensors should be strategically placed throughout the garden.

Lastly, make sure your electroculture equipment is always in top shape by inspecting and cleaning it frequently. To ensure the longevity of your electroculture setup, it is essential to replace any broken or worn-out components.

Safety Precautions and Best Practices

Extreme care must be taken when working with electroculture equipment. Wear protective equipment such as gloves, non-conductive shoes, and safety glasses at all times to avoid injury. Make sure your electroculture setup is far away from any sources of water, as electricity and water are incompatible.

Before making any alterations to your electroculture setup, make sure the power is off or the voltage generator is unplugged to prevent getting shocked. Regular inspections for signs of damage, wear, and malfunction are essential for ensuring the continued security and reliability of any given system. Commercially available electroculture equipment must be set up, used, and maintained in accordance with the manufacturer's guidelines.

Equipment Storage and Care

Your electroculture tools will last longer and perform better if you keep them out of the elements and out of direct sunlight and high temperatures when they're not in use. If you want to get the most out of your gear, you need to keep it clean and well-organized. In order to maintain their accuracy, monitoring devices like conductivity meters and pH meters need regular cleaning, calibration, and storage in accordance with the manufacturer's guidelines.

In case of any breakdowns or malfunctions during the gardening season, having spare parts on hand like extra electrodes, wires, and connectors is a good idea. If you follow these safety measures, you'll have a much easier time keeping your garden's electroculture setup in good working order and getting the best possible results from your plants.

Applications in Vegetable Gardening

Electroculture techniques could boost the yield, reduce the amount of fertilizer and pesticides needed, and make vegetables grown in backyard gardens more resistant to disease and pests. Let's see if we can glean any information about the advantages of applying these techniques to different kinds of vegetables.

Using electrostatic fields and magnetized water irrigation to boost the growth, germination, and nutrient absorption of leafy greens like lettuce, spinach, and kale. Soil electrical conductivity management and plasma agriculture may improve yields, plant health, and root development in root vegetables like carrots, beets, and potatoes.

Electromagnetic field treatment of bean and pea seeds increases germination rates, produces more uniform plants, and makes them more resistant to common diseases and pests. Fruit-bearing vegetables like tomatoes, peppers, and cucumbers can benefit from an electrostatic field application, which improves nutrient absorption and plant health.

Finally, brassicas such as cabbage, broccoli, and cauliflower can benefit from soil electrical conductivity management and plasma agriculture, leading to stronger root systems, enhanced plant growth, and improved nutrient uptake, ultimately contributing to larger, more productive crops. The potential benefits of electro culture in vegetable gardening include higher crop yields, reduced use of chemical pesticides and fertilizers, and improved plant resistance to disease and pests are just a few of the many benefits of electroculture techniques for backyard gardeners. These methods can increase harvests by fostering greater growth and productivity in plants. Electroculture has additional environmental and financial benefits because it strengthens a plant's natural defenses, requiring fewer chemical interventions.

Grown using electroculture techniques, plants make better use of the soil's nutrients and water, resulting in faster growth and better overall plant health. Treatment of seeds with electromagnetic fields, for example, has been shown to increase germination rates, leading to more uniform plantings and possibly higher harvest yields. Careful selection and application of these methods allows home gardeners to simultaneously increase vegetable yield and reduce their impact on the environment

Challenges and Limitations for Home Gardeners

Electroculture techniques have many benefits when used in a home garden, but they also have some drawbacks. Possible negative effects on human health and the environment as well as the need for additional energy resources are just two examples of the many potential drawbacks.

ENERGY CONSUMPTION

Electroculture techniques pose serious environmental risks due to the electricity needed to run the voltage generators and other electrical equipment. The utility costs of home gardeners can skyrocket when this equipment is used frequently or for extended periods. Greenhouse gas emissions and other unfavorable effects on the environment may rise as a result, depending on the energy source.

INFRASTRUCTURE REQUIREMENTS

Home gardeners who want to try electroculture for the first time may have to make a sizable initial investment in supplies. This may require the use of voltage generators, electrodes, and various types of monitoring equipment. It's also possible that homeowners who want to switch to electroculture will have to rearrange their gardens or install new electrical wiring. This may require an extensive preliminary investment and may be technically difficult or time-consuming for some gardeners.

POTENTIAL NEGATIVE EFFECTS ON THE ENVIRONMENT

The excessive use of electrical stimulation may have an adverse effect on the environment by changing the chemical composition or microbial balance of the soil. Production, transportation, and disposal of electroculture equipment and materials may also contribute to resource depletion and pollution.

POTENTIAL NEGATIVE EFFECTS ON HUMAN HEALTH

Not enough is known about the long-term effects of electroculture techniques on human health, and this is something that home gardeners should keep in mind if they use these methods and are exposed to electrical fields and electromagnetic radiation. Some studies have found a correlation between prolonged exposure to specific electromagnetic field frequencies and intensities and potential adverse health effects. This means that any backyard gardener looking to use electroculture techniques needs to be extremely careful to follow all rules and regulations.

Learning Curve and Technical Expertise

There is a learning curve associated with understanding and implementing electroculture, and many backyard gardeners have likely never heard of it. One must learn the specifics of electroculture before attempting to implement it in a backyard garden. This could call for a lot of investigation, trial and error, or advice from professionals.

Conclusion

The new discipline of electroculture holds great promise for the future of vegetable gardening. . The use of electric and electromagnetic fields in gardening may increase plant vitality, increase harvests, and reduce chemical requirements. However, gardens of any size need to think about the space they have available.

The future of electroculture in vegetable gardening looks bright, thanks to ongoing research and development. Improvements can be made to electroculture processes through research into optimum conditions. Most home gardeners cannot afford the high cost and high learning curve of electroculture equipment.

As the need for environmentally responsible farming increases worldwide, electroculture may contribute to a reduction in chemical fertilizers and pesticides. Urban, community, and small-scale gardens may adopt electroculture as interest in organic gardening and eating locally rises.

When combined with vertical farming, hydroponics, and precision agriculture, electroculture can maximize their efficacy. Increase agricultural output while also better utilizing resources and dispersing.

www.ingramcontent.com/pod-product-compliance
Lightning Source LLC
Chambersburg PA
CBHW061123170426

43209CB00013B/1656